Finish & Publish

Also by this Author

How to be Happy (No Fairy Dust or Moonbeams Required)

Getting Unstuck

Reclaim Your Love

Relax and Color

Finish & Publish

WRITING YOUR BOOK AND PUBLISHING WITH AMAZON

Cara Stein

Fire Lizard Press

Contents

Dedication

To authors everywhere, present and future. Keep dreaming, and keep working to make those dreams reality. You make the world a richer place.

Introduction

A survey quoted in the New York Times says that 81% of Americans want to write a book, yet very few people ever achieve this dream. They think about it and talk about it, but they never actually do it.

If you want to write a book but aren't sure how to finish it or get anyone to read it, this book is for you! You'll learn how to write a book, how to make sure it's valuable to your future readers, how to finish it, and how to get it published and into readers' hands. I'll walk you through the same step-by-step process that I've used to finish and publish five of my own books, as well as over 200 books for clients.

You have something to say, and it's not helping anybody if it's just gathering dust in your head or on your hard drive. In this book, I'll show you my simple, proven, step-by-step path to:

- Finish your book and make sure it comes out every bit as good as a traditionally published book

- Structure your book from the ground up to attract the people who need your message

- Build a platform of fans who are eager to buy your next book or product

- Launch your book for maximum impact so that people actually read it

- Earn royalties from your book month after month, even if you don't do any more work

This may sound too good to be true, but it's not. There are plenty of real people who have made this their reality. Chandler Bolt made almost $7,000 in the first month after he released his book.[1] Jeff Goins earned $1,500 in his first weekend selling a $2.99 eBook and went on to build a six-figure business around his books in less than a year.[2] And you've probably heard of Amanda Hocking, the self-published author of young adult fiction who sold nearly half a million books in her first year and went on to land a 7-figure publishing deal with St. Martin's Press.[3,4]

Those bestselling authors aren't magical. There's no difference between them and you, except that you haven't published your book...yet. Only two things set them apart from the millions of people worldwide who want to write a book but never will: knowledge and execution. They know how to write, publish, and market a book, and they take action and *do it*.

---

[1]http://www.businessinsider.com/chandler-bolt-self-publishing-school-2015-4
[2]http://www.businessinsider.com/jeff-goins-entrepreneur-advice-2015-3
[3]http://www.hockingbooks.com/how-i-became-a-published-author/
[4]http://mediadecoder.blogs.nytimes.com/2011/03/24/self-publisher-signs-four-book-deal-with-macmillan/?_r=2

That's it. There's no magic. If you listen to interviews with successful authors, they all say the same thing. That's why I've boiled it down into a system, so you can do it, too.

I've helped dozens of clients finish and publish their books. I know you can do it, too. To help you, I've written this book.

I've also included action steps and guiding questions to help you along the way. I've gathered those all in a handy PDF to make it easy for you.

As a special gift, I've also included the audiobook version of this book, so you can listen on the go.

You can get the whole package at:
https://project-bestseller.com/resources

I suggest downloading it now so you can follow along with the book and map out your publishing plan.

Chapter 1

How the Publishing Process Works

*F*or first-time authors, the publishing process can seem intimidating. That's why I want to start by giving you an overview of the process. When you know what the steps are, it's easier to imagine completing them.

There are two main ways of getting your book published: you can use a traditional publisher or publish your book yourself.

Traditional Publishers

You're probably very familiar with traditional publishers. They're the source of almost all of the books you see in bookstores.

With a traditional publisher, the process goes like this: write a proposal (including the whole book if you're writing fiction), find an agent to represent you, and wait while the agent shops the book to different publishers. Then, if a publisher decides to publish your book, you'll sign a contract and receive an advance. The publisher will probably have changes and edits they want you to make. After that, they take over, getting the book edited, proofread, designed, printed, and distributed for you.

With a traditional publisher, you can expect to earn 10 to 15 percent royalties on hardcover sales, eight to 10 percent on paperback, and 25 to 50 percent on eBooks.[5] However, your royalties will be applied to pay the publishing company back for your advance first. That's called "earning out" your advance. It's only after your book has sold enough to pay back the advance that you'll start receiving royalty payments.

Royalty payments are also delayed a few months to allow for returns. If a bookstore buys 10 copies of your book and then returns eight of them later, the publisher wants to make sure they haven't already sent you the royalties on those eight copies.

There are many advantages to using a traditional publisher. They have the connections and distribution network to get your book into stores across the country. They have staff to handle the editing, design, and production, so you won't have to worry about any of that or put up any initial investment for it. Also, traditionally-published books automatically gain credibility by virtue of the publisher's endorsement.

On the other hand, traditional publishing also has its share of disadvantages. It takes much longer to get a book published through a traditional publisher than if you did it yourself. You can expect it to take at least a year and a half to two years, and some people spend years getting rejection after rejection before they ever get a publishing deal.

[5]https://www.alanjacobson.com/writers-toolkit/the-business-of-publishing/

Also, traditional publishers still expect you, the author, to do most of the marketing for your book. Getting a publishing deal doesn't necessarily mean that your book will sell—you still have to make that happen, and quickly. Publishing companies are always releasing new books, so if yours doesn't sell well in the first few months, it will quickly disappear from their focus.

Meanwhile, your royalties are low, and you give up a lot of control over the book. The publisher will handle the editing and design for you, but that also means that they won't necessarily do it the way that you want them to.

Self-Publishing

On the other hand, if you publish the book yourself, you get all of the control. But that also means you have all of the responsibilities. You can publish your book in a matter of weeks instead of years, and your royalties are much higher. For instance, at the time of this writing, if you publish an eBook on Amazon, you'll earn 70 percent royalties if you set the price in the range of $2.99 to $9.99, and 35 percent outside of that range. For print books on Amazon, you keep 60 percent of the list price, minus printing costs and fees. For example, I have a paperback on Amazon right now at $15.99. It costs $3.25 per copy to print, so I get to keep $6.32, or about 40 percent.

When you publish the book yourself, you also have final say on all editorial and design decisions, and you get to set the price. But that also means you have to make the up-front investment to get the book edited and designed yourself, and you have to determine a good price for your book.

Hybrid Publishing

As an alternative to self-publishing and traditional publishing, hybrid publishing offers a blend of both models. Like a traditional publisher, a reputable hybrid press will be selective about the books they publish and be responsible for the editing, design, and distribution of the book. However, as with self-publishing, the author pays for these services up front and receives a higher royalty on sales.

For authors who don't want to have to learn the publishing business or find and vet editing and design services, the hybrid model can offer the best of both worlds. On the other hand, many companies calling themselves "hybrid publishers" are more like the vanity presses of old. Before signing up with a service, be sure to check their reputation online and ask for sales numbers from past books.

* * *

It's your decision to go for a traditional or hybrid publisher, or publish your book yourself. You may already know which way you want to go, or you may need to think about it.

Also, many authors start with one approach and then switch for later books. Some successful self-publishers—Amanda Hocking, for example—go on to sign traditional publishing deals so that they can focus on writing and leave the rest to the publishing company. Alternatively, some traditionally published authors go on to self-publish their later books so that they have more control over the process and get to keep more of the profits.

I've helped many clients finish and publish their books, and all of them started by self-publishing their books. One client went on to get a traditional publishing deal for his self-published book, but the others have all stayed with self-publishing because that was what made the most sense for them.

Because my experience lies with self-publishing and it's the right choice for more and more people, that's what this book will focus on. However, if your goal is to get your book traditionally published, I hope you'll still find this book helpful. Even if your publisher will be handling a lot of the process for you, I think it's still valuable to know how it works and what needs to happen for your book to be published and succeed.

The Steps to Publishing a Book

Whether the publisher is Penguin, Random House, or you, the same steps are required to publish a book. Here's a brief overview of those steps:

- Writing the book
- Editing the book
- Proofreading the book
- Choosing a title
- Designing the cover
- Selecting formats (hardcover, paperback, Kindle, ePub, audio)
- Formatting the book
- Producing the book (in print or electronic form)
- Releasing the book for sale
- Promoting the book

Of course, each of these steps could fill a book. I can't tell you everything in this book. Instead, my goal is to give you the essential information you need to finish and publish your book without getting bogged down or overwhelmed. You may have heard of the 80/20 rule: 80 percent of the results come from 20 percent of the effort. I want to give you the information you need to complete that most important 20 percent.

The reality of publishing (and life) is that there are many different ways to do things. There's no one right way to publish your book; there are many approaches that will work. Instead of trying to tell you the details of all the different ways you could go about this, including all of the tools you could use and approaches you could take, I'll tell you what has worked in my experience and what I recommend. In addition to my own books, I've helped clients publish over 200 books. I've seen what works and what doesn't. I hope you can use what I've learned to save yourself a lot of trouble and time.

However, if my recommendations don't feel right to you or fit your situation, please disregard them. There is no one-size-fits-all solution. I want you to do what makes sense for you.

Chapter 2

Setting Your Book Up for Success

(What to do Before You Write Your Book)

*T*he biggest mistake most authors make is writing their book before they figure out what it will offer to readers.

If you know from the outset how you want readers to benefit from reading your book, you can craft it as you go along to make sure it achieves that goal. That will make it much easier for your book to deliver an experience that readers want.

The more valuable an experience you can give your readers through your book, the easier it will be to help them, whether it's by informing them or simply entertaining them. And I'll tell you a secret that most people don't know: what we're really doing here is marketing. At its essence, marketing is about helping people meet their needs.

If you're like many authors, you probably feel clueless about marketing. Maybe you even find the idea icky and spammy. You wish you could just write your book and have people automatically buy it, simply because it's good.

If this is how you feel, there are two important things that you really need to know, so please don't skip this section. The first is this: unless you're amazingly lucky, your book won't sell automatically just by virtue of being on Amazon. However, if you can build some sales momentum for your book, Amazon will start promoting your book and actually help you sell more copies. That's a huge advantage for you, especially since Amazon is incredibly good at selling things. With many products, you have to work just as hard for the thousandth sale as for the fifth, but on Amazon, it's more like pushing a car downhill. Once you get it moving, it gets a lot easier.

Another thing I want you to know is that you don't have to sell your soul to sell your book. A lot of marketing is designed to try to make people want something they don't actually want or need so that they'll buy it. That's why marketing has a bad reputation. But not all marketing is like that. If you have something people actually want and can use, then marketing your product is simply the process of helping those people find what they want. That's how I want you to approach the marketing for your book.

To see how this works, think about the last time you bought a book. Why did you buy it? If you read it and liked it, weren't you glad you bought it?

This approach works for fiction and non-fiction. When I buy a fiction book, it's because I want to read a good story. It's hard to find the books that I'll really enjoy among all the others, so if someone can help me find more of those, I'm happy about that. If I find out that an author I like has just released a new book, that's not spam to me—it's great news! It's similar with non-fiction. If I hear about a book that can help me solve a problem I have or learn a new skill, I'm not annoyed to hear about it—I'm delighted.

Since your book will offer something of value to readers, then you owe it to them to let them know about it. You'd be doing them a disservice if you didn't. And that's how I want you to approach the marketing for your book: not as selling or pushing, but as helping your future readers get what they want and need.

How can you do that? The first step is to decide from the beginning what your book will offer to readers. What change do you want to inspire in a person as a result of their reading your book?

The Transformation You offer Your Readers

For non-fiction, it's probably pretty obvious what your book will offer. Perhaps you'll introduce your readers to new information, or you may help them discover something important about themselves. You may walk them through a process or show them a new way of looking at things.

For example, Michael Port's *Book Yourself Solid* provides all of the information necessary to take readers from vague business knowledge and the desire to sell services, to having a profitable, sustainable service business. Steven Pressfield's *Do The Work* provides information to help people realize what's holding them back. It takes procrastinators and wannabes, and helps them transform themselves into practicing artists.

The book you're reading now provides the information you need to go from an aspiring writer to a published author. That's the transformation.

Now, of course, no book can actually transform any reader.

That's the reader's job. But you can provide the information, inspiration, and motivation that make the transformation possible.

For fiction, the transformation you offer is probably less concrete, but it's still there if you look for it. What kind of story are you telling? What is the message of your story? What experience do you want to give the reader?

If your story touches the heart, that's a transformation. So is inviting readers into a world they would normally never see. Even just giving a stressed-out person a few hours away from reality is a valuable transformation.

For poetry, maybe you show your readers beauty in a way they haven't experienced it before. Maybe you make them laugh. Maybe you make them think.

Whatever it is, your book will offer something to your readers. If you can define that from the beginning, you can make sure your book achieves that goal. You'll have an easier time writing the book, and when it's finished, you'll know how to market it in a way that helps people.

What Will Set Your Book Apart

As you're thinking about what your book will offer, consider what makes a book likely to succeed. According to literary agent David Fugate, traditional publishers look for

1) a fresh, compelling idea in

2) an area with a clear and active audience, that's

3) written by the right author who has both a high degree of expertise and name recognition, and who has

4) the right marketing platform for the book.[6]

The reason publishers look for these elements is obvious: they help books sell. You can use the same elements to help your own book sell. (If you don't have them all yet, that's ok. Hardly anyone has all four elements, especially when they're just starting out.)

First, let's look at "a fresh, compelling idea." As you think about your idea for your book, is it compelling? Does it offer a unique take on something people care about? For example, *West Side Story* is basically *Romeo and Juliet* but in New York City in the 1950s. It's familiar, but with enough of a twist to make it different.

If you tell people your idea, and they immediately say, "ooh," you know you have a winner. If you can't explain it in one sentence or less, keep working on it.

To have a successful book, you also need to write something that people want to read. If you look on Amazon and see that there are already several books on the same topic, that's good. It means there's an audience for your book if you can differentiate it from the ones that are already out there.

One great way to make sure that your book is unique *before* you spend all the time and energy to write it is to look at the competition. Look for books that are similar to yours. Notice their titles and the way they present the material. How will yours be different? Will you focus on one small part of the topic? Will you cover ground that nobody else is covering? Can you include a different perspective?

Read the reviews. What do people like about the existing books? What don't they like? What could your book do better?

---

[6]David Fugate. *The Unconventional Guide to Publishing.* Available here: http://unconventionalguides.com/publishing.htm

What's missing that your book could provide?

If you can't find any competition for your book, that's a red flag. How will you find people to read your book? Can you tie it in to some existing audience somehow?

The last two criteria in the list are less about the book and more about you. Don't worry—you don't have to be famous or have thousands of fans before you can sell your book, although that would certainly make it easier!

Right now, I want you to think about why you're the person to write this book. What unique experiences do you have? What perspective can you lend? What information can you provide that's not already out there? If you have official credentials, so much the better, but life experience counts, too. Sometimes just being able to explain a complex subject in an approachable manner is enough.

Finally, publishers look for name recognition and a marketing platform. If you're like most people, you probably have neither. That's ok. You can start building your name now, so that when you finish your book, you will have fans waiting to read it.

Setting Up Your Marketing Platform

For many new authors, it's tempting to put off this step as long as possible and just focus on writing. I've done the same thing myself. Creating the book is the exciting part, so of course you want to focus on that.

Here's why I recommend starting your marketing platform now, even if you don't want to:

- If you don't want to do it now, you're probably not going to want to do it in a few months, either. Waiting doesn't buy you anything.

- It's not going to seem any easier later. In fact, it will be harder because you'll have less time.

- It takes time to build an audience and gather fans. If you start now, you'll have them when it's time to launch your book and you want to get those first few sales and reviews. They can also help spread the word about your book.

This doesn't have to be complicated. In fact, I recommend keeping it as simple as possible: an email list or a Facebook fan page. You just need a way to gather your fans.

As you go about your life and talk to people, you will bump into some who turn out to be interested in your book. If you have no website or mailing list, those people slip through your fingers, and you can't help them. But if you set up a simple place for them to go and learn more about you and stay informed, then you can help them. Remember, it's not about making people want something they don't want or need. It's about helping the people who do want or need what your book will offer.

There are a few different ways you could approach this. One simple way is to build a Facebook fan page for yourself as an author. Set up the page, use it to explain what you're working on, and invite your family and friends to like it. Get some business cards printed up, and as you run into people and talk about your book, hand out the cards to people who express interest. This is a very simple, low-effort way to gradually build a fan base.

Another method is to set up a basic website and email list.

This approach is more involved than setting up a Facebook page, but it's more professional. It shows the world that you're serious.

Also, unlike a Facebook page, you own your website and email list. If you want to contact your fans at any time, you can. With a Facebook page, you'll probably have to run ads in order to get your fans to actually see your posts, and you're at the mercy of any changes Facebook may choose to make in the future.

Think about this, and be real with yourself. What are your goals for this book? Do you want to help people? Earn income? Attract clients? Build your authority? Get on Oprah? Or do you really just want to write the book and maybe show it to a few family and friends?

If you have professional or income-based goals for the book, it's worth taking the time to set up a website and an email list. One very easy way to do that is to use WordPress.com and pay a small fee to remove "wordpress.com" from your website address. You can use MailChimp for your email list—it's free for up to 2,000 subscribers. If you're intimidated by doing this yourself, hire someone. If you use an existing website design instead of having your site custom designed, you should be able to get this done for $100-500. (See the Resources section for more details on this.)

On the other hand, if you're writing mainly for the sake of writing and don't really care about the outcome, it's still worth setting up a Facebook page, simply so you have somewhere to send people who express interest. There's nothing more frustrating than talking about your book and having someone say, "Oh, I'd love to read it when it comes out!"—and knowing you can't do anything about it.

Either way, set up something for your fans, and then keep in touch. Send them a message every now and then—once a month at the very least—so they don't forget about you. If you're writing non-fiction, you could occasionally send them information or articles on your topic. Or, you could talk about your progress on the book. People love behind-the-scenes looks at creation in progress.

Action Steps

- Get clear on what your book will offer your readers. How do you want people to be different or feel different as a result of reading your book?

- Based on that, who is the ideal reader for your book? What are their interests, likes, and dislikes? As you picture someone who would find your book exceptionally helpful and valuable, who do you imagine? What does this person look like? How old is he/she? What websites or magazines would he/she read?

- Identify the fresh, compelling idea for your book. Test it out on a few people and see how they react.

- Explain to yourself why you're the person to write this book. What experience or unique perspective do you offer?

- Research similar books that have already been published. Read their descriptions and reviews. What do people like about these books? What are their complaints? What will set your book apart?

- Get clear on your personal goals for this book. What's

the most important outcome you want to see from publishing this book? (ex. income, fame, changing the world, clients, authority, the joy of writing)

- Set up a website and email list or a Facebook fan page. Invite your friends and family to join—no pressure. Just present it as an option if they want to support you and follow your progress.

- Print business cards and carry them with you wherever you go. Whenever someone expresses interest in your book, hand them a card so they can join your fan page or email list if they want to.

- Write an initial draft of what will go on the back cover of your book. Even if you're only publishing in eBook formats, you'll still need the same sort of description that helps people decide to buy your book—it will just go on a website instead of the back cover. The reason I recommend writing a first draft of this now is that it will guide you to make the book helpful (and thus easy to market). If this was the most helpful book in the world for your ideal reader to accomplish the transformation you've set out, what would the back cover say about it? What are the most appealing things you can highlight about this book so that people will want to buy it? Figure it out now, and then write the book to fulfill these promises.

You can download all of these action steps and questions in one handy PDF at https://project-bestseller.com/resources.

Chapter 3

Writing Your Book

(and actually finishing!)

*F*or many people, the idea of being a published author is
enchanting, but the idea of actually writing a book seems
impossibly overwhelming and intimidating. Where do
you start? How do you ever finish such a big task? And how do
you make sure you don't just end up making a big jumbled
mess?

Writing a book may be big, but it's actually pretty simple.
This chapter will show you how to do it so that you never have
to feel lost or stuck, and you can see your progress adding up
as you work toward your goal. That will help you stay motivated
to the end (or should I say The End?).

Any task can seem intimidating if you don't know how to
do it or if you try to take on too much at once. If you think
back to the other big things you've accomplished, you couldn't
have done any of them in one shot, right? Whether it's running
a marathon, getting a degree, climbing a mountain, or starting

a business, if you think about the whole project and try to do it all at once, it seems impossible. But if you learn how it works, discover the steps required, and start doing it one step at a time, you eventually get there.

Even for something simple like following a new recipe or doing the dishes after a dinner party, the whole thing can seem overwhelming until you take it one step at a time. It's the same way with writing a book. Can you write a whole book today? Probably not. But can you write one scene of a story or 1,500 words on one very specific topic? I'm betting you can. And if you do that over and over, that's how you write a book.

Now, I don't recommend sitting down and writing a bunch of unrelated scenes or sections. You can do that if you want to, but you'll probably have a lot of cleanup work to do at the end. Instead, it's a lot more efficient to plan out where your book is going first.

Planning for Fiction

If you're writing fiction, you probably already have some idea of the characters and story you want to tell. How much more detailed do you need to get?

There are two schools of thought on this. Some people like to do some character sketches, identify the setting and the concept for the story, and let the story take them where it wants to go. When your characters start doing things you had no idea they'd do, it's a magical experience.

On the other hand, you may find it easier to do more planning before you start writing. There's no right or wrong way to do this—it's just a matter of what works best for you.

For me, if I have some characters and a theme, but I don't

really know where the story is going, I never finish. But if I have a plan for the narrative arc, what the main points of conflict will be, and how the story will end, it's a lot easier. That's the only way I ever finish. My characters still surprise me sometimes, but I know where the story is going overall, so I never feel that writers' block dread of a blank page.

If you decide to plan your story, think about the structure of a hero's journey.

- In the beginning, we see the life to be left behind.

- Something happens to push the hero to change or move.

- The hero probably clings to his or her old life at first. Then it becomes obvious that things need to change.

- There's often a guide who helps the hero, and another character who encourages him or her to keep things as they are.

- The hero goes through a series of challenges and obstacles, learning and getting stronger through each one.

- Finally, the worst thing imaginable happens and the hero is pushed to his or her limit.

- The hero overcomes the challenge and steps into his or her new self.

- The loose ends are tied up, and the story is resolved.

For your story, it may help to set down these elements in advance. You'll also want to get clear on your main character. Who is he or she as a person? How will readers identify with him or her? What archetype does he or she represent?

What other characters need to be in the story? What are they like? What does the story demonstrate or say?

You don't need to create a full-scale, detailed outline of every single thing that will happen in your story, but it does help to nail down these points in advance. You may even want to specify one to three main things that happen in each chapter. (For a really interesting look into how this works for one team of writers, check out *Fiction Unboxed* by Sean Platt and Johnny B. Truant.)

If you need more detailed information on how to plan your novel, I recommend reading *Bestseller* by Celia Brayfield. For more direction on the spontaneous approach, I recommend *No Plot? No Problem!* by Chris Baty. Another great book on how to plan a novel is *Tactical Storytelling: One writer's guide to finishing the first draft* by C. Steven Manley.

Planning for Non-Fiction

For non-fiction, there's less magic involved. You'll still want to include stories if you can, because they'll help your readers stay interested and relate to your material. But non-fiction can stand without that if the information is interesting and useful.

To plan a non-fiction book, here's the process I recommend.

- Brainstorm all of the topics, ideas, and concepts you want to include in your book. You could do this as a mind map or as a simple list.

- Start grouping the topics and ideas together in logical chunks by topic or theme.

- Think back to what you want this book to offer readers. How do you want them to be different after reading this book?

- Arrange the topics or themes in the order that seems most effective for helping your reader achieve that goal.

- Arrange the ideas within each topic in an order that makes sense and supports the overall progression of the book.

- Look at the list from the perspective of the book as a whole. Are there any bare spots that need to be fleshed out or augmented? Any crucial information you're missing? Any parts that really don't belong in this book and need to be taken out?

- Go back through your ordered list of topics, subtopics, and ideas. Some elements are probably more important than others, and some are parts of larger themes. At this point, you can determine the hierarchy. Which points are chapter titles? Which points will become sections within those chapters, or points within those sections? Revisit the order and rearrange things if necessary.

- Look at the level of detail you have. Is this detailed enough that you feel confident that you could write each section? If not, keep breaking it down until you do.

Once you have this plan laid out, writing the book is mainly a matter of researching and writing each section. You'll probably need to add an introduction to the beginning and a conclusion at the end, but at this point, you have an outline for your book. Now all you need to do is fill it in.

What if you don't have an idea?

Ideally, you've decided to write a book because you have an idea that just won't leave you alone. To be honest, all of my ideas for books have basically shown up and sat on my chest, meowing relentlessly until I did their bidding. No wait, that's my cat—but the behavior of ideas is very similar.

But maybe you don't have an idea taking over your life. Maybe you can't think of any ideas at all right now. If that's the case, think about why you want to write this book. Are there any ideas hidden in your reason?

For example, if you want to write a book because you know it will help you gain recognition as an expert and attract clients to your business, your idea lies in that. What topic do you want to demonstrate your expertise in? What information would your clients beat down your door to get? That's what you need to write about.

Another approach for finding non-fiction ideas is to think about what you're most interested in. What are you good at? What do you do for fun? What subject have you studied so deeply that everyone in your household is tired of hearing about it? Write about that.

On the other hand, if you want to write fiction, look in your life for interesting or funny premises. Make a habit of asking yourself, "what if...?" What if you somehow ended up with your 20-years-younger self as the apprentice to your current self? What if you could stop time whenever you wanted? What if the South had won the Civil War? What if that couple behind you in the grocery store checkout line had secret superpowers?

Another option is to make up some characters and a setting, and just start writing and see what happens. This is the approach recommended by Chris Baty, one of the founders of NaNoWriMo (National Novel Writing Month). It's probably less efficient than starting with a plan, but if you really want to write a book, it's far better to write than to sit around waiting for an idea to turn up. Even if you don't end up using a lot of what you write, it can still pave the way for an idea that will work.

Writing the first 10,000 words of a doomed novel was enough to pull me out of a deep depression, even though I knew from the beginning that I would probably never do anything with this particular book idea. You never know where writing may take you.

Choosing Your Tools

Before you sit down to write your book, you need to decide what tools you're going to use to write it. Will you write longhand on paper with a fancy pen? Take your iPad and Bluetooth keyboard to your favorite park bench? Use your laptop on the couch?

Assuming you're not writing longhand, there are many choices for tools you can use when you write your book. One choice is Microsoft Word. For most people, it's familiar and readily available, so it's the choice that makes sense. If you don't have Microsoft Word, OpenOffice offers a word processor that's very similar, and it's free.

Another option that's worth checking into is Scrivener. Scrivener is a program that was created specifically for writers. In addition to a word processor, it has a lot of extra features that can help you organize your book, reach your writing goals, and format your book once it's written. It's an inexpensive program (currently $49), and it has a free trial. It also has the ability to import and export into Word, so if you don't like it, you can always switch back to something more familiar. If you have time, it's worth checking out. I've never met a writer who tried Scrivener and didn't become a fan.

The important thing is choosing the tools that will support you along the way. If you're not sure what to do, just use what you have. Don't let the quest for the perfect writing software delay your writing.

Setting Yourself up to Finish

Armed with your plan and your tools, you're ready to begin your own hero's journey to finish your book. At this point, you want to do everything you can to ensure that you'll finish your book. So, what makes the difference between people who finish and people who don't?

If you listen to published authors, you'll hear a few common themes. One is the idea of going pro. That means you set a schedule, and you stick to it whether you want to write at that moment or not.

You may have heard the quote attributed to Somerset Maugham about whether to write on a schedule or when inspiration strikes: "I write only when inspiration strikes. Fortunately, it strikes every morning at nine o'clock sharp."

You don't have to write at nine o'clock sharp, and you don't have to write every single day, but if you don't schedule time to write and stick to that schedule, you probably won't finish your book. So decide now: when are you going to write? Go through your schedule and carve out at least half an hour a day. More is better, because you can take advantage of your momentum, but for most people, it's not realistic to expect to write regularly for more than two or three hours in a session.

Some people recommend writing absolutely every day. That way you never lose momentum. Personally, I find that I get burned out on any project if I don't schedule weekends off. I may still work on the weekend anyway if I want to, but if I feel like I have to, then I start hating the whole thing.

In fact, I much prefer a sprint to a marathon. When I had a job, I'd take a week of vacation time, neglect all but my most essential responsibilities, and just write like mad for nine days straight in attempt to finish a complete draft before I had to go back to work. If you're a fast writer and you write short books, this can be a very effective approach. On the other hand, if you're writing an epic saga, a slow but steady approach is far more sustainable and probably makes a lot more sense.

Do what works for you, and don't be afraid to experiment a little to find what works best. The important thing is to schedule some time to write, and then show up and write. Unless the house is on fire, don't let anything pre-empt your writing time. I can say from experience that if you let this happen once, you open the door for it to happen again and again. If you want to finish your book, your writing time is non-negotiable.

Setting Your Own Deadlines

For many people, it also helps to have deadlines. You've probably noticed in your own life that most things happen at the last minute, and things with no deadlines tend not to get done.

By setting deadlines for yourself, you can help yourself stay on track and finish your book. It helps if you can tie the final goal to something immovable in real life so that you can't just blow it off. For example, maybe you want to finish your book in time to take copies to an upcoming literary festival. Maybe you want to finish it before your next birthday so you can show it off to your family and friends. Maybe you'll follow the NaNoWriMo plan and write your entire book in the month of November. Maybe you want your book launch to coincide with your business's anniversary or you want to finish before the cruise you're taking next spring so you can use the trip to celebrate. Anchor points like these can really help to ensure that you finish on time.

Another approach is to look at the amount of work, estimate how long it will take, and set a deadline based on that. For example, if you plan to write one section per day and your book contains 57 sections, you know you'll need about 60 writing sessions (when you add in the introduction and the conclusion). If you're writing five days a week, it will take you 12 weeks, so count out a date 12 weeks from now.

Whatever you choose for your deadline, circle it on your calendar and think of it often. Post it where you'll see it all the time. Finishing your manuscript is a big accomplishment, so plan what you'll do to celebrate.

For most people, it also helps to break the project into smaller milestones so you can make sure you're on track. For example, you may want to aim for a specific word count for each session. If you're using Scrivener, Word, or Open Office, the software will count the words for you. Scrivener will even show you a color-coded progress bar based on the goals you've set.

Another approach is to decide what section or scene(s) you'll write in each session. Or, you may set target dates for each chapter.

Whichever approach you take, you can help yourself achieve the goal by making your progress as visible and addictive as possible. This can be as simple as a checklist of all of the parts of your book, which you check off after each session so that you can see the completed parts adding up. Or, it could be a progress bar of current word count vs. estimated final word count. Whatever you use, make it easy to tell at a glance that you're making progress and whether you're on target or not. That will help you play to win.

In addition to setting a deadline for the writing, I also want you to set a deadline for publishing the book. Make it one to three months after your deadline for finishing the manuscript. Schedule in a vacation for the following week.

This serves two purposes: it gives you a hard deadline, which will help you avoid the finish-itis that plagues so many new authors when it comes time to press the "publish" button, and it will ensure that you take some time off to rest and recharge after you finish this project. You deserve it.

Making a Commitment

Another crucial step in finishing your book is committing to finishing your book. If you don't decide with 100% certainty that you *will* finish this book, it will be easy to quit when the going gets tough. And for any project worth doing, the going always gets tough at some point.

If you don't really want to write a book, that's fine. But if you do, make an agreement with yourself right now. It could look something like this:

I, _____, commit to writing my book

and finishing by this date: _____. I realize that life will offer many obstacles and temptations along the way, but writing this book is important to me. I will honor my schedule and see it through to the end.

[sign and date]

If you're serious about your book, I encourage you to actually print out a commitment statement, sign it, and hang it up where you'll see it often. You may have to put other parts of your life on hold temporarily until you finish your book. If your book is more important to you than those other things, you'll defer those things and finish the book. If it's not, you won't. It's not right or wrong either way; it's just a matter of what's most important to you.

Becoming a Writer

For many people, writing a book requires a mental shift in the way they see themselves. Up to this point, you've been a person who has not written a book. Now, you're transforming yourself into someone who has. In the process, you'll grow as a person.

As you work on your book, you can approach it in one of two ways. You can go the self-effacing route and say things like, "I'm trying to..." or "Oh, that's just my little pet project." You may do this without thinking about it, in attempt to stay humble and not claim to be a writer or an author before you've really earned the title. In my experience, this approach results in errands and appointments pre-empting writing sessions, friends and family utterly lacking respect for the project, and increased difficulty in ever getting the book done.

The other approach is to see finishing your book as inevitable and step into your new identity now. As of your first writing session, you are a writer. Writers are people who write—that's it. And as of now, you are the author of your forthcoming book, [insert title here].

If it makes you more comfortable, think of yourself as an author minus six months (or however long you expect it to take to finish your manuscript), but think of yourself as an author. That shift in mindset will help you finish your book.

Also, you need to respect your project and take it seriously. If you don't, no one else will, either. When I was writing my first book, I was constantly angry and resentful that people would schedule other things during my writing times or interrupt me and expect me to pay attention to them instead of writing. But then I realized that I was treating the book the same way myself.

Of course, I still had other responsibilities. We all do. But those other responsibilities don't have to monopolize every minute of every day. They can get along without you for half an hour while you write.

If you find yourself experiencing a lot of pushback from people around you about your writing time, it may indicate that you aren't taking the project seriously enough yourself. In my case, once I decided that the book was my number-one project and my writing time was sacred, everyone else quickly fell into line. I just had to get my attitude right first.

Writing to Finish

As you sit down for the first writing session of your new book, you may find yourself staring at a blank page and freaking out. If that happens, don't worry about it. Just start writing.

This is the key: don't worry about writing well. As much as you can, turn off your internal editor for the duration of the first draft and don't judge your writing at all. Just write.

In particular, don't sit down for your first session and try to write the perfect first sentence or an entrancing introduction. Now is not the time for that. In fact, you may want to start writing in a later section, just to take the pressure off. Pick a scene or topic where you know exactly what you want to say, and start writing.

After you've written the rest of the book, the introduction will be much easier to write. You'll have already gone through your book's journey with your readers (even if they don't know it yet), so you'll feel comfortable talking to them and bringing them into the beginning of the book. Meanwhile, just start somewhere and write.

Once you get some momentum going, it all becomes much easier. Sometimes, it can feel like the words are writing themselves, and all you have to do is type quickly enough to capture them. Other times, it feels like a slog.

It's important to realize that it's that way for everyone. If it feels like you're walking through tar just to get the next paragraph down, or everything you write one day is clunky and embarrassing, don't worry. That's normal—even for the most experienced and revered writers. Remember, Ernest Hemingway said, "The first draft of anything is shit."

Your only goal is to write your shit. Get it all down. You can fix it later. It's much easier to turn shit into something good than to turn nothing into something, so keep writing, even when it sucks.

A Word on Self-Discipline

Depending what else is going on in your life, how passionate you are about your book, how much you like writing, how quickly your book progresses, and many other factors, you may find the writing stage easy or difficult. Whatever you find, I recommend relying on self-discipline as little as possible. Self-discipline only goes so far, and anything you can do to avoid needing it is something that shifts the odds in your favor.

How can you write a book without relying on self-discipline? Use other, stronger tools as much as you can. One of those tools is routine. If, every day, you get up in the morning, eat breakfast, take a 15-minute walk, pour yourself a big cup of coffee, sit down at your writing desk, and write, then it becomes habit. You don't think about it. You don't have to make yourself do it; you just do it.

Another tool is passion. Keep reminding yourself why you're excited to write this book. What do you love about the story or the subject matter? How do you anticipate the book changing your life and that of others? Keep these things in the front of your mind to drive you on.

Another very powerful tool is accountability. It's a quirk of human nature that most people will do things to impress others, help others, or avoid embarrassment, even when they'd never do those same things just for themselves. Enlist the help of a coach or accountability partner to help you stay on track. Some people even place bets with their friends, so they'll lose money if they don't finish.

Think about what will help you stay on track and stay motivated. Set up as many tools and aids as you can to make it easier for yourself to finish.

Action Steps

- Plan your book, whatever this means for you. It may be a few character sketches, or it may be a detailed scene-by-scene or topic-by-topic outline. If you're not sure how much structure you need, give yourself a little more. That way, you won't get stuck later, wondering what to do next.

- Schedule your writing sessions. Mark them in your calendar and don't let anything pre-empt them.

- Set your final deadline and milestones between then and now. Circle your final deadline on your calendar and remind yourself every day that you're going to finish your book by then. Also set a deadline for publishing your book and schedule a vacation the week after.

- Make a scoreboard or progress chart and post it where you can see it.

- Commit to writing your book and finishing it by your deadline.

- Begin thinking of yourself as the author of your forthcoming book.

- Get a coach or accountability partner to help you stay on track.

- Turn off your internal editor.

- Start writing. Write shit if necessary. Show up for every writing session, and write. Repeat until you finish. Track your progress on your progress chart as you go.

- Don't forget to drop your fans a message now and then.

- When you finish your manuscript, celebrate! Most people never get this far, so do something big.

You can download all of these action steps and questions in one handy PDF at https://project-bestseller.com/resources.

Chapter 4

Preparing Your Book for Publication

You've written your manuscript! Congratulations! Now you're an author, and nobody can take that away from you. The next step is getting your book ready for publication.

Choosing Formats and Venues

There are more options than ever for publishing your book. As a self-published author, you can release it in print formats (paperback and hardcover), eBook formats (Kindle, ePub, and PDF), and audio. You can publish it in serial form on your own website. Or you can do all of these and more.

How do you know which formats to choose? That depends on your goals for your book and where you are now. To understand the formats available for your book, it may help to think about venues first.

Publishing Venues

For most self-published authors, most sales come from Amazon. To be more specific, most indie authors receive the vast majority of their sales by selling a Kindle edition on Amazon. If you're not sure which venues and formats to choose for your book, start with a Kindle edition. You can always release other formats later. Even traditional publishers often release a hardcover book and then publish a paperback edition a year or two later. Also, by publishing the Kindle edition first, you can use the royalties from your book to help pay for formatting and expenses, if you choose to release your book in other formats.

In addition to Kindle, you can use Amazon to sell your book in paperback, audio, and even hardcover if you choose.

For eBooks, other outlets include Barnes & Noble, Apple's iBook Store, Kobo, and many more. For these venues, you'll need an ePub edition of your book. EPub is another eBook format that's very similar to Kindle.

You could set up an account with each of these sites, or you could use a distribution service. The two main distribution services are Smashwords and Draft2Digital. Smashwords has been around longer and has partnerships with more venues, but most of those venues are obscure and don't result in significant sales anyway. Meanwhile, Draft2Digital is more pleasant to use and offers a better eBook conversion process.

If you choose either of these services, you can set up one account with them, and they'll distribute your book to Barnes & Noble, Apple, Kobo, and many other sites. They do take a cut of the royalties, but in most cases, it's worth it to get your book into so many venues without having to manage all of those accounts yourself.

Another option is selling your books through your own website by setting up eCommerce software or using a simple shopping cart service such as E-Junkie. (See the Resources section for more information.) You can even sell your print books this way if you want. If you don't want to be responsible for shipping the books yourself, you can use Fulfillment By Amazon. This service allows you to store your books in Amazon's warehouse and have Amazon ship the orders to customers for you.

For audiobooks, the main outlets are Amazon, Audible, and iTunes. If you use Amazon's ACX service, you can get your book into all three venues at once.

Finally, if you publish a print edition, you can try to sell it to bookstores. For most self-published authors, it's very difficult to get into bookstores beyond your local area, but if this is important to you, it's worth pursuing.

If it's a specialty book, you may also be able to get it into related specialty shops. For example, if it's a children's book, you may be able to sell the print edition in toy stores or gift shops. If it's a book about dogs, you may be able to get your local pet-related shops to carry it. If it's a book about local history, you may be able to get it into the gift shops of local tourist attractions.

As you think about your book, you probably have some ideas for which venues you want to use to distribute it. The venues you plan to use will determine which formats you'll need.

EBook Formats

As I mentioned earlier, in my experience, most self-publishing authors sell the majority of their books as eBooks in Kindle or

PDF format.

Kindle is Amazon's special eBook format. It's based on simple HTML (the markup language used to format websites). (Don't worry—you don't need to learn HTML in order to publish your book.) Kindle books can be read on Kindle devices. They can also be read on most computers, tablets, or smartphones once the Kindle App is installed.

PDF is a format that almost everyone can read—most computers and tablets have some sort of PDF reader installed. PDF gives you a lot of control over how your book looks, regardless of the device used to display it.

If you have a business with a large following, you may find that publishing the book in PDF and selling it from your own website will make you the most money. If you add a few other resources and market your book as a guide, rather than an eBook, you can charge $10-50 for the package. By selling it on your own website, you avoid Amazon fees, so you get to keep almost every penny of that. (You will probably have to pay transaction processing fees and some kind of shopping cart service charge. If you want to do this, you can use PayPal to process the transactions for 2.9 percent plus 30 cents per transaction within the U.S., and E-Junkie provides shopping cart service for $5/month.)

However, if you don't have a large, established audience, Kindle will probably be where you get the most sales. Even if you do have a big audience, Kindle may be your best bet. When your existing fans buy your book, Amazon will notice those sales and start promoting the book to others. This is a great way to get your book in front of people who might never have encountered your work before.

Regardless of your current audience, Amazon is a great partner in selling your book. Amazon was the first company to start making serious money on eBooks, and they're still dominant in this area. If you're only releasing your book in one format, Kindle is the format I recommend. There are no printing costs, you get 70 percent royalties if your book is priced from $2.99 to $9.99, and Amazon is unmatched in selling eBooks. If you can make your book start selling, Amazon will throw their weight behind it, too, so you can make many more sales than you could any other way. Even if you don't care about the money, more sales mean your book is in more hands, helping more people.

Another eBook format is ePub. This format is very similar to the Kindle format, and it can also be read on most tablets and other devices. If you want to sell your eBook on Barnes & Noble, Apple's iBook Store, Kobo, or any of the other online bookstores besides Amazon, it will need to be in ePub format. Fortunately, ePub and Kindle are very similar. If you hire someone to format your book, they'll often do both formats for little or no extra charge.

Print Formats

The main options for releasing your book in print are paperback and hardcover. Depending what type of book it is, you could also consider spiral binding, saddle stitch (stapling), or other types of specialty binding. If it's a cookbook or other book that needs to lie flat, this is something to consider.

For most books, though, paperback is the way to go. It's much less expensive than hardcover, and paperback books are lighter. Paperback editions are also offered by more printing companies than hardbacks.

Should you do a print edition of your book? Like everything else, that depends on your situation.

As recently as 10 years ago, if you wanted to publish your book, you had to contract an offset printer, get your books printed, and store them until they sold. You've probably heard stories of people who spent thousands of dollars to get their book printed, only to end up with a garage full of books that never sold.

That's not how it is any more. You can still get your book printed by offset printing if you want to. It costs less per copy to do it that way, and the quality is very good. But another option is Print On Demand.

With Print On Demand, you send an electronic version of your book to a printing company, usually in PDF format. Then, when someone orders your book, the printing company prints a copy and ships it directly to the customer.

The great thing about this option is it eliminates almost all of the up-front costs of offering a print edition. You don't have to order several thousand copies of your book in advance; all you have to do is get it formatted, upload it, and see if anyone buys it. Your customers will pay the printing costs when they order their copies of the book.

Most of my clients sell far fewer copies of their books on paperback than eBook formats. But offering a paperback edition may still be worth doing. Here are a few of the advantages:

- There's nothing quite like the experience of holding a print copy of your book in your hands, with your name on the cover. EBooks are great, but they can't give you that.

- Offering a paperback edition sets you apart from the amateurs and internet marketers on Amazon, who generally offer only a Kindle edition. In contrast, if a book is traditionally published, you can count on it to be available in at least one print format (paperback or hardcover).

- Not everyone has joined the eBook revolution. Some people will only buy and read print books.

- If you have a print book, you can do book signings and other events to generate publicity for it.

- A print book makes an incredible business card. If part of your goal for your book is to gain exposure and attract new clients, imagine walking up to prospects and handing them a copy of your book. That makes a lasting impression. You can expect to pay about $3-5 apiece for copies of your own paperback.

- Offering a print edition also anchors the price of your book at a higher point. If you have only a Kindle book, buyers will see only the Kindle price. But if you offer a paperback edition, Amazon will show the print price, cross it out, and show the Kindle price below it. As a result, your Kindle book always looks like a bargain.

There are several companies that offer Print On Demand services, but the three most commonly used are Amazon's KDP (Kindle Direct Publishing), IngramSpark (Lightning Source), and Lulu. If you've heard of CreateSpace, that used to be Amazon's Print On Demand service, but it has since been incorporated into KDP.

I recommend Amazon's KDP for most people. They're the easiest and highest-royalty way to get a print book on Amazon. They don't charge a setup fee, and they don't charge a fee for changes to your files. That means you can upload your book, order a proof copy, change it if you want, release it, and list it for sale on Amazon, all for $5 or less (the cost of printing the proof copy).

When someone orders your book, the buyer pays the printing costs, shipping costs, and fees. The book is automatically printed and shipped directly to them, and you collect the royalties. For most self-publishers, this is the clear choice.

Another option is IngramSpark. If you've heard of Lightning Source, it's the same company. Lightning Source is intended for publishing companies, whereas IngramSpark works with independent authors.

IngramSpark charges a small setup fee, and they also charge a fee if you change your files. Their system is also considerably less user-friendly than Amazon's. So, why would you use IngramSpark?

If you want to offer a hardcover edition of your book, IngramSpark can print them on demand and get them on Amazon for you. Amazon's KDP doesn't offer a hardcover option.

Also, if you want to sell your books in brick-and-mortar bookstores, you won't be able to with KDP. Book retailers expect to be able to return unsold books, and KDP doesn't allow that. Retailers also expect a higher wholesale discount than KDP offers. For that reason, if you want to get your book into bookstores, you'll need to work with IngramSpark.

For most self-published authors, getting bookstores to carry your book is a long shot, even with IngramSpark. But it's basically impossible with KDP.

IngramSpark offers lower royalties with Amazon than KDP, so if you do this, I recommend using KDP for sales through Amazon and IngramSpark for other sales. To set this up, buy your own ISBN (we'll talk about this in more detail in chapter 4). Then set your book up in KDP first and make sure you have it exactly how you want it (since changes are free on KDP), and DO NOT enable Expanded Distribution on KDP. Once you're sure you have the final version of the book, then set it up on IngramSpark as well. That will get it into the catalog that bookstores use to order their books. In IngramSpark, you'll want to choose these options:

- Allow returns (otherwise bookstores won't order books, so it's not worth bothering to put the book in Ingram-Spark at all). You can have returned books sent to you for an extra fee, or you can have them destroyed. As you're making this decision, consider the price of getting a new copy of the book printed. If it's about the same as the disposal fee, it makes more sense to have the books destroyed and just order new copies if you want them.

- Use the standard discount (55 percent). This is the discount wholesalers and distributors get (from your list price). Bookstores may buy from distributors. In this case, the distributor keeps 15 percent and gives the bookstore a discount of 40 percent off list price.

You'll also want to print the list price on the back cover near the bar code for the ISBN. (We'll cover this in more detail in chapter 4.) Otherwise, the only way for shoppers in stores to know the price of the book is for the bookstore to put a sticker on the book—a step they may not want to bother taking.

The third main company that offers Print On Demand services is Lulu. Lulu offers more different binding options than the others. If you want to offer a saddle stitch (stapled) or spiral-bound edition, Lulu will print those on demand for you. But for standard paperbacks, Lulu's printing prices are higher, so you'd be better off using KDP and/or IngramSpark.

Other Formats

You might also consider offering your book as an audiobook. The audiobook market is growing, and offering this format will give you the chance to reach people who can't read or don't like reading.

Again, most people sell way fewer audiobooks than eBooks. You may want to wait and see if your book sells well in other formats before deciding whether it's worth doing an audio edition.

If you do decide to offer your book on audio, I recommend using ACX, which stands for Audiobook Creation Exchange. ACX is another Amazon company, and they'll list your audiobook for sale on Amazon, iTunes, and Audible. You can record it yourself or hire a narrator to do it for you. (Note: if you decide to do it yourself, make sure you use a good microphone, make a high-quality recording, save each chapter in its own file, and edit out all of the mistakes.) ACX can also help you find actors and producers for your book. Some of them will even work for a share of the royalties with no fee up front.

Next Steps

Once you've chosen your venues and formats, it's time to think about the appearance of your book, specifically the cover design and editing. How you approach these will depend on your goals and resources. At the most basic level, you could take your manuscript straight to Amazon, set up an account at kdp.amazon.com, upload your manuscript, use their cover-design tool to create a cover, and publish your book within 24-48 hours.

I don't recommend doing that yet, though. Here's why.

You've written your book for a reason, and you've spent a lot of time and energy to finish writing it. You've probably written when you were tired, pushed through when you thought you couldn't go on, missed some fun times, and consumed too much coffee and sugar. Maybe you even made your spouse or family mad a time or two when they wanted your attention and you kept working on your book.

You pushed through and finished, despite all obstacles, because your book is important to you and has something to offer the world. It's worth taking a little more time to present it in the best possible light.

As you've browsed the Kindle books on Amazon, you've probably noticed a few that look like they were slapped together by an amateur, and not a very sophisticated one. Because publishing for Kindle is free and relatively easy, anyone can do it, and lots of people have—including plenty of scam artists who just push out "books" to make a quick buck. Your book needs to stand apart from the amateurs and scam artists so that people trust you enough to buy it.

How can you separate your book from the Kindle junk? There are two main factors: cover design and editing. Get the highest quality you can afford for both.

When you've spent weeks or months writing a book, it's easy to get so caught up in the project that you forget that you're the only one who knows what's inside it. For everyone else, it's just another book among thousands that they might consider buying. You have to show them that your book is the one they need, or they'll never buy it. That starts with the cover.

Cover Design

Most people couldn't tell you what goes into a professional book cover design, but most people can spot an unprofessional one a mile away. If your cover doesn't look completely professional, you've immediately blown all credibility.

Beyond simply looking professional, the cover also needs to be appealing and convey at a glance what's inside the book. The purpose of the cover is to attract potential readers enough that they'll flip the book over and read the back cover (or click on the Amazon link and read the description). To do that, it needs to be enticing, it needs to visually communicate the genre of your book, and it needs to capture the feel of the book and what it's about. All of this needs to take place in two seconds or less, before the reader moves on to look at something else.

People always say, "Don't judge a book by its cover," but the reason that's an expression is because people *do* judge books by their covers all the time. Other than keeping rain off the pages, that's what book covers are for. Your book will certainly be judged by its cover, so if you can only afford to spend money on one thing, spend it on getting the best cover design you can.

Some people will recommend using sites like Fiverr or other cheap ways to get book covers made. Some publishing platforms (including KDP) even offer tools to help you design your own cover. You can try these approaches, and you may luck out, but in my opinion, it's worth spending the money to hire a professional cover designer.

Look for someone who specializes in book cover design. If they specialize in books of your genre, so much the better. If you know other self-published authors and you like their book covers, you can also ask for recommendations.

Look through designers' portfolios. Do you like their past work? Does it seem like their style would be a good fit for your book? Do the examples in their portfolio make you want to pick up those books and find out more?

Expect to pay $200 to $500 or more for a professional cover design. Some designers will present multiple concepts for you to choose from, and then develop one final design based on your feedback. This way, you have a better opportunity to tailor the cover to what you want and make sure you like it. This is your book, and the cover should showcase it.

If you're planning to offer a print edition of your book, make sure your cover designer knows that up front. Be prepared to pay a little more, because a print book will need a back cover and a spine as well as the front cover, which is all you need for eBook formats. Also, if you're planning to produce an audiobook edition, have your designer create that at the same time. Audiobook covers need to be square, whereas print and eBook covers are normally rectangular. It's best for the same designer to do them all at the same time so that they look consistent.

Editing
The other important factor that separates professional books from unprofessional ones is editing. Everyone needs an editor,

even the best writers. Professional editors hire other editors to edit their work, and there's a good reason why: you can't see your own mistakes. Once you get too close to a project, your mind plays tricks on you and shows you what you "know" is there, not what's actually there. You need someone else to spot your mistakes. Of course you'll want to revise your manuscript and make it as good as you can, but then you need to turn it over to someone else.

You may be thinking, "Hey, wait a minute! I've seen plenty of published books full of mistakes. What about *50 Shades of Grey*? That series has sold millions!"

That is true. If you're happy with your book the way it is, it's not my place to tell you what to do. I still recommend getting someone else to edit your book, though. Here's why.

A good editor doesn't just fix commas and missing words. (That's proofreading, which is only the last stage of editing.) A good editor helps make your book stronger. They'll point out awkward phrasing and unclear passages. They'll help make your book flow better. They'll spot misused words and expressions. They'll polish your style and make your book shine, even if you're not the greatest writer by yourself.

There are a few different types of editing that you should know about. The highest level is developmental editing. A developmental editor helps with the overall structure and organization of the book. Does the story make sense? Do the chapters follow a logical progression? Is the writing persuasive? Is anything missing?

You may or may not need a developmental editor for your book. If you get stuck or feel like your book isn't as good as it could be and you don't know why, a developmental editor is the person to help you.

The next level of editing is more detailed. You may hear this called line editing or copyediting—different people use these terms in different ways. At this level of editing, the editor polishes your writing. They'll make suggestions for rewording sentences that are clumsy or unclear. They'll help you improve clarity and flow. They'll catch excessive passive voice, repetitiveness, and other correct but grating constructs. They'll help you make your chapter titles and headings as effective as possible.

Finally, at the lowest level, you have proofreading. Proofreading is simply checking for errors of spelling, punctuation, and basic grammar. If you've got a comma in the wrong place, a proofreader will catch this for you. On the other hand, if your sentence is awkward but technically correct, that's beyond the scope of proofreading.

You may think that none of this matters—who really knows all the rules well enough to notice your mistakes anyway? But you need to think about it from a reader's perspective. The people who buy your book will do so under the assumption that it's a high-quality, professional book. If it's full of typos and errors, they feel like they've been tricked. That makes them feel stupid, which makes them angry, so they strike back by leaving scathing reviews. You've probably seen this on other people's book listings.

More importantly, even tiny editing mistakes distract readers. If it's fiction, mistakes take readers out of the story and remind them that they're reading a book. If it's non-fiction, mistakes can make your meaning unclear. They can also make readers wonder if you made as many mistakes with your facts as you did with your writing. Either way, these seemingly inconsequential mistakes hinder your book's ability to deliver the benefits you intended.

If you really want to present your book in its best possible form, it's worth hiring a professional book editor. You may be tempted to ask family or friends, and that's better than nothing, but remember that family and friends just want you to be happy. Unless they're extremely devoted and detail-oriented, they'll probably just tell you that your manuscript looks fine or point out a few simple errors while missing many more. If you can't afford a professional editor, please at least hire a local grammar nut to proofread your manuscript.

Many people call themselves editors but really only do proofreading, so make sure you ask exactly what type of editing is involved before you hire anyone. To get an idea of how much you can expect to pay a professional editor or proofreader, check out the Editorial Freelance Association's list of editorial rates here: https://www.the-efa.org/rates/

Formatting Your book

Once your book has been edited, you're almost ready to publish it. You just need to prepare your manuscript in the appropriate formats for the venues you've chosen. That's what I mean by "formatting." The rules on this will vary from site to site, so make sure you read the specifications if you're going to do this yourself.

Kindle and ePub

To prepare your book for release in the Kindle and ePub formats, there are a few approaches you could take. One is to format the book by hand. If you're not familiar with HTML, I don't recommend this. Another option is to use an automated conversion process. For example, you can try uploading your manuscript as a Word document and let Amazon convert it for you. This may work if your book is just straight prose with no fancy formatting. However, in most cases, something will be messed up in the conversion.

Another option is to use Scrivener. Scrivener is a program designed for writers, and it offers many export options, including Kindle and ePub. I haven't used this process enough to draw conclusions about it, but for novels and other books with simple formatting, it may be all you need.

Finally, you could hire someone to format your book for Kindle and ePub for you. If you hire a professional, look for a track record of satisfied customers. Also, make sure the conversion process includes all formatting, links, in-book navigation, and a table of contents. You want the "Go to..." menu to work and readers to be able to skip to the next section seamlessly. (Automatic conversion tools often miss these two features.)

PDF

To prepare your book for release as a PDF eBook, you can use Scrivener, layout software such as Adobe InDesign or Quark Xpress, or a word processor such as Open Office or Microsoft Word. Depending which tool you're using, the option to create a PDF may be called "export" or "save as," or you may find it under the "print" function. If you don't have the ability to export in PDF format, there are also many websites that will convert a Word document to a PDF free.

Print

To prepare your book for print, you'll generally need two PDF files: one for the cover, and one for the pages. All graphics should be at least 300 dpi, and all type should be 100% black. Otherwise, your book will come out looking fuzzy.

You can hire a book designer to format your book for you. Your cover designer may offer this service, or he or she can recommend someone. If you can't afford a book designer, you can tackle the formatting yourself.

Scrivener offers export options for print as well as eBook formats. It's also possible to format your book in Word or OpenOffice and export it to PDF. If you decide to do that, KDP offers templates that you can use to help you with the formatting. You can get those here: https://kdp.amazon.com/en_US/help/topic/G201834230

I'm used to professional design tools, so I can't say much about formatting a book in Word (except pack a lot of patience!). If you do decide to go that route, here are a few tips to help make your book look professional:

- Look at traditionally published books and pay attention to the details of how they're laid out. Notice the margins, the typefaces, the page numbers, and the headers or footers.

- Choose a serif font such as Caslon, Palatino, or Times for the body text. Use full justification for your body text (smooth margins on left and right). Print out a few test pages at actual size to make sure the type is a reasonable size compared with traditionally published books. (Some programs will automatically stretch or shrink your work to fit an 8.5"x11" page—not helpful in this situation! Look for a setting that says "Actual Size" or 100%.)

- Add a title page, copyright notice, table of contents, and any front matter you want to include (Introduction, Foreword, Dedication, etc.).

- Use information at the top or bottom of the page help the reader stay oriented within the book. For many books, the book title is printed at the top of the left page, and the chapter title is printed at the top of the right page. Or, you may see the section title at the top of the left page and the chapter title at the top of the right page. In either case, these are known as "running heads." Page numbers will often appear in the margins next to these headers. Another option is to put them at the bottom of the page.

- Chapters always start on a right-side page. If you need to, insert a blank page at the end of the previous chapter to move the new chapter to a right-side page. For the first page of a chapter, you'll usually see the chapter title in larger type, then the body text starting about halfway down the page. There will be no running head on this page, and the page number often moves to the bottom of the page.

- Right-side pages are always the odd-numbered pages.

- If a page doesn't have any text or graphics on it, it also shouldn't have a running head or page number—leave it completely blank.

- You shouldn't have a blank right-side page in a book unless it's a notes page or other specialty page. In that case, make sure it's clear that it's intentional. (For example, write "Notes" at the top of the page.)

There are many more details for formatting a book, but if you follow these rules, your book should look pretty good.

For the cover, you'll need a file that includes the back cover, spine, and front cover. Your printing company will print this file onto a large piece of paper, which will become the physical cover of the book. Have your book designer prepare this file for you when he or she designs the cover. The requirements for print are stricter than for eBooks, so it's best to have your print cover done at the same time as the original design. You may run into problems if you have it done after the fact. The cover is the most common place for errors and printing problems, so it's wise to use someone with experience.

For an audiobook, you'll need the cover file (square), and you'll need all of the audio files.

Buying ISBN(s)

An ISBN is a unique identifier for your book. ISBN stands for International Standard Book Number. In the U.S., these numbers are issued by a company called Bowker. You can also buy them indirectly through other companies.

Each ISBN uniquely identifies not only the book, but also the format it's published in. Therefore, the same book can have multiple ISBNs if it's published in several different formats. For example, if a book is published in Kindle, ePub, paperback, hardcover, and audio editions, it may have five different ISBNs—one for each format. You can't reuse the same ISBN for multiple formats, even for different formats of the same book. The ISBN has to uniquely identify the format as well as the title. This way, when a customer wants to buy the book, he or she can be sure of getting the desired format.

However, that doesn't necessarily mean you'll need five ISBNs for your book. You may not even need one. It depends which formats and venues you choose for your book.

If you're publishing your book only on Kindle and/or your own website, you don't need an ISBN. For your website, you can use whatever identifier you want, and for Amazon, you can use Amazon's own numbering system: ASIN (Amazon Standard Identification Number). When you upload your Kindle book, Amazon automatically assigns it an ASIN, and you're ready to go.

For eBooks published on other sites, the rules vary. Many sites use their own internal number systems, just as Amazon does with their ASIN. But some sites require you to use an ISBN.

You'll also need an ISBN for each print edition you offer, and you may or may not need one if you offer your book in audio format.

There are a few different approaches to acquiring ISBNs, and some things you should know. Some sites—including KDP, Draft2Digital, and Smashwords—offer free ISBNs that you can use when you publish or distribute your book through them.

Of course, everyone loves something that's free! The drawback here is that you can't use that ISBN to sell your book on other sites (even if it's the same format). For example, if you use a free ISBN from KDP for your paperback, you can't use the same ISBN to publish that paperback through another service (such as IngramSpark).

The other drawback is that, in exchange for the free ISBN, you can't control what's shown as the publisher of your book.

For example, if you use KDP's free ISBN, when your book appears on Amazon, it will show "Independently Published" for the publisher. It's up to you whether you care about that or not. Most buyers might not notice or know what this means, but to anyone who is knowledgeable on book publishing, it immediately indicates that your book was self-published (and you didn't spring for your own ISBN).

The other option is to buy an ISBN. In the U.S., you'll do that through a company called Bowker. Currently, Bowker sells one ISBN for $125, but they'll sell you 10 for $295. If you're planning to do a whole lot of books, you can get 100 for $575. Obviously, there's a big difference between buying one at $125 and buying 100 for $5.75 apiece! If you expect to write a lot of books and offer them in multiple formats, buying ISBNs in bulk is definitely the best option.

Aside from price and flexibility, another factor to consider when buying your ISBNs is how the ownership will be recorded. If you buy your ISBN(s) directly through Bowker, you (or your company) will be the publisher of record. If you get an ISBN through KDP, the master records will still associate that ISBN with KDP. Many people recommend only buying directly from Bowker for this reason.

Personally, I have a hard time imagining anyone looking through the master records to find out whether your ISBN was originally sourced through KDP. If someone wanted to offer you a publishing deal, they would have to already know that you were self-published, and why would anyone else care? But I wanted you to have all the facts so you can make your own decision.

If you do buy your ISBN from Bowker, they will also try to

sell you a variety of other services, including barcodes. In my experience, you won't need to buy any barcodes. KDP and IngramSpark will generate them for you for your paperback. Most other services don't require them. And, if you do need one, there are free services online that will generate them for you. I've included a few links in the Resources section, but you can also find them by Googling "Free ISBN barcode generator."

To understand an ISBN barcode, the first section represents the ISBN, and the second section represents the price. (If there's only one section, it's just the ISBN.) Here's a sample from the Free Online Barcode Generator at http://www.terryburton.co.uk/barcodewriter/generator/

ISBN 978-1-56581-231-4

9 781565 812314

52250 >

In this example, the ISBN is 978-1-56581-231-4. That's what's encoded in the first part. The second part shows the price. In this case, the code is 52250, which means $22.50. The 5 on the beginning represents U.S. dollars, and the rest is the price (without the decimal point). A first digit of 6 represents Canadian dollars, 4 is for New Zealand dollars, 3 is for Australian dollars, and 0 and 1 represent British pounds. If you see a code of 90000, that means the price is unspecified.

As mentioned before, if you plan to sell your book in stores, you'll want to print the price in human-readable form (ex. $20.50) above the barcode as well. If you're just selling it online, you don't need to do that. Online customers buy the book before they have a chance to receive it and see the cover.

Action Steps

- Decide which venues you want to publish your book in.

- Based on your venues, which formats will you produce your book in?

- This is a good time to check in with your fans. You can start building anticipation for your book by letting them know you've finished the first draft. Update them again as you go through the publishing process.

- Hire a cover designer. If you're doing paperback and/or audiobook formats, get those done at the same time as your eBook cover design. Your paperback cover can't be finalized until you have a final page count to determine the width of the spine, but it can be close.

- Hire an editor to polish your manuscript and make it even better than your best writing. If you can't afford that, at least hire a proofreader to go over your manuscript and catch the mistakes you can't see.

- Hire someone to format your book, or format it yourself.

You can download all of these action steps and questions in one handy PDF at https://project-bestseller.com/resources.

Chapter 5

Publishing
Your Book

*O*nce you have the book formatted, publishing it is basically a matter of uploading the formatted files to the various sites. However, most of my clients seem to get stuck at this point. I think there are two main reasons why: they're afraid of making a mistake, and they're even more afraid of changing the world.

For some reason, people have a lot of resistance to taking the final step to finish something, even if it's something they've been dreaming about and working toward for years. The last step of publishing a book can be a big mental hurdle for many people, because it represents a shift in the state of the universe. Before, you are not a published author. After, you are. If you have any feelings of unworthiness or doubts about how people will receive your book, those will probably come up and get in your way at this point.

I've seen this over and over again. Clients will spend all of the time, money, and energy to get their books finished, polished and ready to publish... and then they'll sit there for months and not publish. In my experience, the number-one thing that gets people past this sticking point is a deadline.

That's why I recommended setting a publishing deadline before you even finish writing your manuscript. If you didn't do it then, do it now. Set up a launch party or some other event so that you need to have your book available on a certain date. The only people I've seen not get stuck before hitting the "publish" button were the ones who were freaking out about not getting their books in time for some event. The people with deadlines sail over this hurdle and hardly even notice it.

To give you an idea of what's involved in actually publishing your book, I'll walk you through the process for the formats that are likely to account for the majority of your book sales: setting up your Kindle book and your paperback in KDP.

Publishing on Kindle

To publish your book, you'll need to set up an account at Kindle Direct Publishing: http://kdp.amazon.com. This account will be tied to your Amazon account. Before you can publish your book, Amazon will require some bank account and tax information. That's to make sure they can pay you properly and not get themselves or you in trouble with the IRS.

Once you have an account, log in and you'll see your Bookshelf. In the beginning, there will be nothing here, but later, this is where your books will be listed.

To create a new book, you'll click "Create New Title." Then, you'll have two pages of questions to answer. Amazon changes the exact format of this periodically, but currently, here's the information you'll need to fill out on the first page:

- **Language** (what language was the book written in?)

- **Book Title**

- **Subtitle** (optional)

- **Series Name** and **Series Number** (optional—skip this unless the book is part of a series)

- **Edition number** (optional—you'll probably skip)

- **Author** (that's you!)

- **Contributors** (This may also include co-authors, editors, illustrators, or other contributors if you had any. Usually, it's just you, though.)

- **Description** (This is where you'll put the text that would go on the back cover of a paperback. People read this to decide whether or not to buy your book, so make sure it's compelling and persuasive. You are allowed up to 4,000 characters, and you can use simple HTML to format the text if you want. If you do that, take out all the line breaks or Amazon will add a big gap at each one and your description will look wonky.)

- **Publishing rights:** public domain or you own the rights (If you wrote the book, you own the rights.)

- **Keywords** (up to 7, optional. These help people find your book, so use all 7. If you were trying to find a book, and your book was exactly what you wanted to find, what search terms would you use? That's what you want to put here. A "keyword" can actually be a phrase. Separate the keywords or phrases with commas. There's no need to put your title here—from what I understand, Amazon already uses the title, subtitle, series, and author fields as search terms, so don't waste keywords by repeating these.)

- **Categories** (Pick two from the list, based on the genre and content of your book—this will help people find your book.)

- **Age and Grade Range** (optional—you'll probably skip these unless it's a children's book.)

- **Pre-order** (Release the book now or make it available for pre-order—this just depends on when you want to release your book)

At this point, you can click "Save as Draft" or "Save and Continue." Either way, the information you've entered will be saved, and your book will not be published yet. If you choose to continue, you'll be taken to the next page. Here's what you'll see:

- **Digital Rights Management (DRM)** (You can choose yes to try to protect your book from piracy, but DRM doesn't actually stop anyone who wants to pirate a book, and it makes life more inconvenient for people who actually buy the book. It's up to you, but I recommend not enabling DRM.)

- **Manuscript** (If you hired someone or used Scrivener to format your book, this will be a .mobi file. Amazon also allows you to upload other file formats, including Word, HTML, ePub, PDF, RTF, and plain text for automatic conversion. If your book has very simple formatting, this may work. Otherwise, it will probably be messed up. But automatic conversion is free, so it's worth a try if you want to.)

- **Cover** (Upload your cover design here, in .jpg or .tif format. The file must be at least 625 pixels on the shortest side and 1,000 pixels on the longest side. Amazon recommends 1,600 pixels wide by 2,560 pixels high. The file should be in RGB format (which it probably already is) and less than 50 MB. If there's a problem with either of these, you'll get a warning message, so don't worry if you're not sure.)

- **Preview** (Here you'll have a chance to flip through an online preview of your book. You can also download Amazon's Kindle Previewer app if you want. Look through the whole book and make sure the formatting looks right before you publish it.)

- **ISBN** (optional—you'll probably skip this. If you fill it in, make sure the ISBN you place here is one that you purchased, and don't use the same one for any other formats.)

- **Publisher** (optional—you can skip this or make up a name for your imprint. As a self-publisher, you're basically a tiny publisher, so you can name your publisher identity if you want to. Just don't pick anything that's trademarked by someone else. You can check this by searching the U. S. Patent and Trademark Office or your country's equivalent.)

Again, you can click "Save as Draft" or "Save and Continue."

Either way, the information you've entered will be saved, and your book will not be published yet. If you choose to continue, you'll be taken to the next page. Here's what you'll see:

- **KDP Select Enrollment** (This is a program that allows you to offer your book free for up to five days out of every 90 days. It also offers you other promotional opportunities, including Kindle Countdown Deals and enrolling your book in Amazon's Kindle Unlimited subscription service. The drawback is that you have to offer your eBook exclusively on Amazon while it's in this program. You can sell a paperback edition elsewhere, but you can't sell a PDF, Kindle, or ePub version of it anywhere else. If you're only planning to sell your eBook on Amazon, you may as well enroll in this program and get the benefits. If you want to sell it on other sites, this program isn't for you, but it may still be worth enrolling for the first 90 days after release.)

- **Territories** (worldwide or individual territories—if you wrote the book, you own all the rights, so choose worldwide.)

- **Royalty and Pricing:**

  - **Royalty option:** 35% or 70% (You can only choose 70% if you price your book in the $2.99 to $9.99 range. In most cases, that's the smart choice.)

  - **List price on Amazon.com** (Again, you can set any price, but $2.99 to $9.99 is probably where you'll make the most money. Not only are royalty rates double in that range, but that's also the price range that most people are willing to pay for a Kindle book.)

- **List price on the Amazon sites for other countries**
  (Amazon will calculate these automatically based
  on your U.S. list price, and then you can change
  them individually yourself if you like)

- **Kindle Matchbook** (If you have a paperback edition,
  this option will allow you to offer a discount if people
  buy your book in both paperback and Kindle. I recommend enabling this option. Your Kindle book costs you
  nothing to give to someone, so if offering them a discount or a free copy makes them more likely to buy the
  paperback edition, that's a win for you.)

- **Kindle Book Lending** (This will allow people to lend
  your book to others after they buy it. If they do lend it
  out, the other person gets access to the book for two
  weeks, during which time the purchaser can't access it.
  Then it automatically reverts to the purchaser. I recommend enabling this. If someone wants your book
  enough to borrow it, there's a good chance they'll want
  it for longer than two weeks and end up buying it. If
  they don't, you've lost nothing.)

At this point, you can "Save as Draft" again if you want to come
back later, or you can click "Save and Publish" to publish the
book.

Once you click "Save and Publish," your book will go under
review while someone at Amazon checks to make sure it meets
the Kindle publishing standards. This can take up to 48 hours,
but in my experience, it's usually done in 12 hours or less. Then
you'll receive an email informing you that your book has been

approved and published! You'll get a link and be able to see it on Amazon.

This is an exciting moment! If you see any errors, go back and correct them now, but if it looks good, tell all of your family and friends. They'll be proud and excited for you, and they may give you your first few sales!

Publishing your paperback

The process for publishing your paperback through KDP is very similar and requires a lot of the same information. To do this, you'll go to your KDP dashboard. If you've already set up your Kindle book there, it will also have the option to create a paperback. Click **Create Paperback** and follow the steps. You'll find that KDP propagates some of the information from the Kindle edition and pre-fills it here for you.

The first page should look very familiar—it's all information you've already given for the Kindle edition. Once you check the information and make sure it's correct, you can click "Save" if you want to come back later or "Save and Continue" to keep going.

The second screen deals with the ISBN, printing specifications, and content. Here's what you'll need to enter:

- **Print ISBN**

  - **Get a free KDP ISBN** (This is free, but "Independently Published" appears as your publisher, and you can't reuse this ISBN elsewhere.)

  - **Use my own ISBN** (If you bought your own ISBN from Bowker, you'll choose this option.)

Note: once you save your ISBN choice, you can't change it.

- **Publication Date** (You'll leave this blank unless your book has already been published in the past.)

- **Interior & Paper Type** (If the inside of your book includes color, choose color interior with white paper. However, this will increase your printing costs significantly. Otherwise, it's black & white on white paper or black & white on cream paper. White vs. cream paper is a matter of personal preference.)

- **Trim size** (This is the size your book will be when it's printed. The default is 6"x9" but don't stick with that unless that's the size your pages were designed for. Depending on the genre, your book may be 5.5" x 8.5", 6" x 9", or one of many other sizes. If you did the page design yourself, you had to choose the page size when you chose a template or set up your document. If you paid someone to design your book, ask him or her if you're not sure.)

- **Bleed Settings** (Unless you're doing an arty book that has graphics going all the way to the edge of the page, you'll choose No Bleed.)

- **Paperback cover finish** (Matte or Glossy—again, a matter of personal preference.)

- **Upload paperback manuscript** (This will be a PDF with each page of the book as a separate page in the file (as opposed to spreads, which show a pair of pages together as one page).

- **Book Cover** (This is the PDF from your cover designer that includes the back cover, spine, and front cover all on one page for printing.)

- **Book Preview** (Once you've entered everything else, KDP's automated system will generate a preview of what your book will look like once it's printed. It will also point out any red flags it spots, such as images that are too low in resolution, pages the wrong size, or text printing too close to the margin. If it finds errors, you'll want to correct them and upload the corrected files before submitting the book for publication.)

The Print Previewer will also give you the opportunity to download a PDF proof of the book. I recommend downloading the PDF and looking through it, too.

If you're on a tight deadline to release the book, I also recommend printing the PDF of the interior of the book at this point. People always catch mistakes on paper that they'd never see on a screen. By going through a printout now, you can catch those mistakes and fix them without having to wait for KDP to review your book or print and ship a proof copy. I usually upload the PDF directly to Office Depot's Copy & Print service. They can print all of the pages and have them ready within a few hours. (Again, make sure you choose "actual size" or "100%," not "scale to fit page" so that you can see all of the elements at their actual size.) The copy and print center will often have a paper cutter you can use to trim the pages to size if you want to.

You can also get your PDF printed in person, but it usually costs a bit more. Either way, it's worth it to look through a physical copy of the book at this point, especially if you're up against a deadline. Catching mistakes now can save a lot of time.

Once you approve the files for your book, KDP will show you a summary of the options you've selected. It will also show you a calculation of printing costs for different Amazon marketplaces.

Once you click Save and Continue, you'll go on to the distribution and pricing page. Here's what you'll enter:

- **Territories** (worldwide or individual territories—if you wrote the book, you own all the rights, so choose worldwide.)

- **Pricing & Royalty** (This is where you'll set the list price for the book, and KDP will calculate your royalties on sales from Amazon.com and other markets. As with the Kindle edition, the pricing in other countries will be calculated automatically, and then you can change it for individual countries if you like.)

- **Expanded Distribution** (If you're planning to offer your book to bookstores through IngramSpark, DO NOT check this box. Otherwise, you can check it, and your book will become available to bookstores and libraries to order, although as mentioned earlier, it's unlikely that they will.)

- **Request for printed proof** (Currently, this isn't a button or anything, just a link to click, so it's easy to miss. I always recommend ordering at least one printed proof before the book goes live.)

Once you've finished all that, you'll submit your book for review. The review process may take up to 72 hours. You'll receive an email when the book has been reviewed. If there are any errors, you'll be notified. Meanwhile, you'll wait for your printed proof to arrive in the mail.

I recommend getting a printed proof for every book. Even if you've been through this process before, there's always a chance that something will go wrong in the setup. I once had CreateSpace make a mistake and print my entire book in dots instead of solid black lines, due to an error they made in processing. If I hadn't ordered a proof copy, I would never have known unless buyers complained... or until I received my first order of 50 books and they were all wrong!

Depending on the shipping speed you choose, it can take up to two weeks to receive your proof copy, but it's usually much less. If you hired someone to design your book, order one for your designer as well. That way, if there is a problem, you can send your designer a copy so that he or she can figure out what went wrong.

Once your proof copy arrives, look through it. Again, this is a time to celebrate! There's nothing like the feeling of holding your book in your hand and seeing your name on the cover for the first time.

If you see problems, this is the time to correct them. If you make changes to the cover or interior files, your book will go through the review process again and you'll probably want to order another round of proof copies. But if the proof looks good, go ahead and approve it.

Now that you've seen the process for publishing your Kindle and paperback through KDP, you can publish your book just about anywhere. The websites look different, and they put things in a different order, but they all require the same basic information about your book. It's just a matter of walking through the process and answering the questions.

Some people feel intimidated by this process. If you find yourself feeling this way, just take it slow and answer one question at a time. Even if you do make a mistake, there's no need to worry. Everything except the ISBN can be changed later if necessary.

Registering your Copyright

In the U.S., you automatically own the copyright to your work as soon as you produce it. You don't need to register it in order to own the rights to it. You don't even need to put a copyright notice on it. If you made it, you own it.

However, I still recommend registering the copyright for your book. It's easy to do, it's not very expensive (fees are currently $35 to $55 to register a book), and it gives you an official record of ownership. In the event of a lawsuit, if you've registered the copyright within five years of publishing the book, it's considered *prima facie* evidence in a court of law. If you register the copyright promptly, you may also be eligible to collect statutory damages and attorney's fees if you ever have to go to court over the rights to your book. Chances are, you'll never need any of this, but if you do, there's no substitute.

You may have heard that you can mail yourself a copy of your manuscript and leave the envelope sealed, thus using the postmark as proof of the date when you created it. Here's what the U.S. Copyright Office has to say about that:

> The practice of sending a copy of your own work to yourself is sometimes called a "poor man's copyright." There is no provision in the copyright law regarding any such type of protection, and it is not a substitute for registration.

To register the copyright for your book, you'll go to

Copyright.gov and set up an account. You'll fill out a simple form and send in your registration fee. Depending which formats you're publishing your book in, you may be able to submit an electronic copy of the book, or you may have to mail two copies to the copyright office. It's a very simple process.

Action Steps

- Buy ISBNs if needed.

- Consider writing to some of your fans to offer them advance review copies of your book.

- Upload and publish your book.

- Register your copyright.

You can download all of these action steps and questions in one handy PDF at https://project-bestseller.com/resources.

Chapter 6

Selling your Book

You've achieved your dream and published your book. Congratulations! At this point, you may be wondering: now what?

If you're like most people, what happens next is that you'll obsessively check the publishing sites countless times a day to see how many copies of your book have sold. You'll probably also stagger around feeling a little lost without your book to work on. If that happens, don't worry—it's normal, and it will pass.

Everyone is different, but in my experience, nothing gets done the week after a huge accomplishment like finishing a book. If I try to work, I'll basically sit at my desk and drool on my keyboard, no matter how hard I try to get myself to do something. That's why I recommend taking a week off after your publish your book if you possibly can.

After that, your next big project is selling the book. Of

course, this part is optional, and most authors never do it. But if you want people to read your book, you need to get the word out and help them find it.

If you set up an email list or Facebook fan page back in chapter two, this is where you'll be really glad to have it. You know that your fans want your book, so they'll probably be your first sales. They're also a great source of reviews.

But if you didn't do it, don't worry. There are plenty of other ways you can promote your book and get the word out.

This is the part that stumps most authors, but if you listen to bestselling authors talk about what they did to sell so many books, you'll hear the same things over and over again. They all work on getting positive reviews as soon after publication as possible, and they all promote their books with some combination of ads, guest posts, press releases, interviews, and messages to their fan base. They all stage the biggest launch they can to make a big splash when their book first comes out.

There's no magic here. The only difference between someone who ends up on the New York Times Bestseller list versus people like you and me is scale. We can do all of the same things they do. We just have fewer connections and probably a lot less staff working on marketing.

No matter who you are, you need the same elements to sell books. You need a great cover and effective sales copy (that's your book description). You need positive reviews, and you need a way for people to hear about your book. Let's talk about how you can get those things.

We've already discussed how important your cover design is. That's why I strongly recommend hiring a professional designer, even if you don't spend a penny on anything else for your book.

Strengthening your Book Description

For your description, the key is to show people why they want to buy your book. Remember, we're not trying to make people buy something they don't want or need. We're trying to help people who do want what we offer.

If you're not confident that your description is the best it could be, take the time to study what works. Look at books that are similar to yours, and read their descriptions or back covers. Pay attention to how they make you feel. Which ones make you want to buy the book? Look at those more closely. What parts do you find most compelling? What common themes do you notice? How are these writers arousing your curiosity and interest, and making you want to dive into the book?

For example, I helped two of my clients write book descriptions for their memoirs. Before I started writing, I went to Amazon and looked at the top-selling memoirs. (To find the best-selling books in a category, look at any book in that category. Scroll down to the book's Amazon Best Sellers Rank, which is currently located at the bottom of the Product Details section. If the book is selling at all, you'll see where it ranks in one or more categories. If you click on any of these categories, Amazon will show you the top 100 bestsellers in that category.)

As I read the descriptions for these books, I paid attention to how I felt. Any time I felt a pull toward the book, I noticed what phrase had triggered that feeling. Some of the themes I noticed were: inspiring stories, situations that I wouldn't be likely to experience any other way, behind-the-scenes looks at someone else's life, success stories that also show the bumps and bruises along the way, and people achieving their dreams. Both of my clients' memoirs included all of these elements, so I made sure to highlight them when I wrote the book descriptions.

The exact elements you'll use will vary from genre to genre, but if you look at similar books that are selling well, you'll discover what elements you need for yours.

Another basic copywriting technique is to highlight the benefits of what you're offering. Luckily, you know exactly what your readers will get out of your book—you figured that out in chapter two! If your book is fiction, this will be more subtle, but if it's non-fiction, make a bullet list of the crucial things the reader will learn by reading your book. Phrase them to build curiosity. (For example, I could have made one of the bullet points for this book "why you need to figure out the transformation your book offers before you start writing," but that doesn't inspire much curiosity. Instead, I might say something like, "the big mistake most authors make that keep their books from ever selling—and how you can avoid making this mistake." Phrasing like that automatically makes people wonder what the mistake is and whether they're already making it.)

By putting these elements in a bullet list, you make a visual statement that your book offers a lot of value. You also help the reader stay interested and keep reading your description.

Writing an effective book description is an art, and it's a different skill from writing a book, but it can be learned. If you'd like to read more on copywriting, I recommend *Write to Sell* by Andy Maslen. If you're selling fiction, I recommend *How to Write a Sizzling Synopsis* by Bryan Cohen. Most authors hate this part, but these books provide a structure to help you do it well.

Getting Reviews

When people are deciding whether to buy a book or not, one of the first things they look for is reviews. If other people have read and liked your book, everyone else who comes along later will feel more comfortable buying your book. Even negative reviews can sometimes help sell your book. If I read a negative review that complains about something I enjoy in a book, it actually makes me more likely to buy the book, not less.

Still, as an author, negative reviews hurt. It feels a lot better to have people like your work, and it's good to start with a few positive reviews if you can. I'm not in any way suggesting that you buy reviews or pressure people to leave positive reviews. Both of those approaches are unethical and against Amazon's terms of service. However, there's nothing wrong with asking for honest reviews from people who are likely to enjoy your book. That's a perfectly legitimate approach, and it's one I recommend.

One place to start is with family and friends. Of course, if Amazon realizes you have a close connection, there's a good chance they'll delete the review.

You may also see some advice to send reviewers a gift copy of your kindle book so their review will appear as a verified purchase. This used to work, but the last time someone I knew tried it, Amazon deleted all of the reviews received this way. I assume that Amazon concluded there was a biased relationship, because the author had given the book as a gift.

Instead, you'll want to email the Kindle or PDF file directly to your reviewer and ask them to mention that they received a free copy of the book in exchange for their honest review.

It's still worth asking your close family and friends to review your book. Just don't be surprised if those reviews get deleted later. If you have some distant friends or close acquaintances who would be likely to enjoy your book, they're even better people to ask for reviews.

If this sounds scary, remember: your goal is to help people. If these people will benefit from reading your book, then you're doing them a favor by offering them a free review copy of your book. They're also doing you a favor by writing you a review, so it's a fair exchange.

To approach this, you'll want to contact each of these people individually. Briefly explain that you've just written your first book. Describe what it's about in three sentences or less, and mention why you think this person would enjoy reading it. Then ask if they'd be interested in a free review copy.

Make it clear that it's OK if they say no, but you'd love their help if they have the time and interest. It may also help to mention a date by which you'd most appreciate the review. That helps people make time to do it, rather than putting it off indefinitely.

As you make these requests, expect about half of the people you ask to say yes, and about half of those to actually write a review. Many people have the best of intentions but simply have too much going on to get around to writing you a review. There may be others who don't really like your book but don't want to leave you anything less than a glowing review. They're helping you, even if they don't write a review.

This is simply part of the process, so aim to be grateful to everyone and not worry about which individuals leave you reviews or what they say. Also, don't get attached to any particular review or your number of reviews. The rules of the game say

that Amazon can take down any review at any time for any reason, and sometimes they do. It may feel unfair, but that's how
the system works.

In addition to friends and family, don't forget your fans.
Many of them will be delighted to leave you a review. You may
want to contact particularly active members of your community
(people who respond to your posts or reply to your email messages) and offer them a free review copy of the book. You can
do this before or after the book officially comes out. As your
fans buy your book, also gently request reviews from them. Let
them know how much that would help you and why, and you'll
probably find that many of them are delighted to help you out
by leaving a review.

Another way to get reviews is to reach out to bloggers and
other writers who share the same interests. Let them know why
you think they'd particularly enjoy your book and offer a free
review copy. Many will say no, but some will say yes. If they go
on to leave a review, be sure to thank them.

You can also look at the reviews for similar books on Amazon. Some reviewers publish their contact information in their
profiles. If you find a reviewer who liked a book that's similar
to yours, see if he or she has a public email address. If so, write
and offer a free review copy of your book. Again, explain why
you think that your book would be of particular interest to this
person.

The more reviews you have, the more credibility your book
will have with potential buyers, so it's worth continuing to chip
away at this project. Over time, you'll accumulate a substantial
collection of reviews for your book.

Getting the Word Out

The other key factor in book sales is marketing and publicity. People need to hear about your book before they can decide to buy it, so it's important to get it in front of as many potential buyers as possible.

It's important to note here that not everyone is a potential buyer. There are plenty of people who would not enjoy your book or find it useful, no matter how good it is. There's no point in getting it in front of those people. Instead, you want to target your ideal readers and get it in front of them as much as possible.

If you need to, go back to your notes on your ideal reader from chapter two. What characteristics does this person have? Where does he or she hang out? What podcasts, blogs, magazines, or other venues could you use to reach him or her? Make a list, and then look for ways to get featured in those venues.

For podcasts, you'll want to approach the host and pitch a reason for him or her to interview you. Look for the intersection between the content of your book and the theme of the podcast. What can you offer that would be of most value to this audience? Podcast hosts always need content, so if you can offer something of value, that's a win for the host and for you. You can also offer a few copies of your book as a giveaway if the host is interested. That's a gift to the audience, and it gives you and the host an excuse to talk about your book.

For blogs, the approach is similar. Pitch a few ideas for guest posts, and make sure that each idea contains some crossover between the theme of the blog and the content of your book. (If you can't come up with any common ground, that's probably a sign that this isn't a good venue for promoting your book anyway.) Again, offer the book as a giveaway if the blogger is interested.

For magazines, you'll want to pitch ideas along the same lines. You may also consider buying ads if a publication is very specifically targeted to your ideal reader. If you can get an ad and an article into the same issue, so much the better.

Also, don't forget your local media, alumni networks, and any relevant professional organizations. Send press releases with any newsworthy angle you can think of: local author publishes book on X, any events you may be hosting, and any hook you can think of to tie in your book with current events or trends.

You'll also want to mention your book on social media. Don't do this so much that it becomes spammy, but any time you reach a milestone or have any exciting news about the book, post about it—especially if you can include pictures.

The people in your network on social media are there because they're interested in you in some way. There's a good chance they'll be interested in your progress and successes as you publish your book. They may even decide to support you by buying a copy or telling their friends. But if they don't know what you're doing, they can't help you.

It's especially important to keep your fans in the loop. They're your strongest supporters and the people most likely to buy your book. If you can help them feel like part of the journey, many of them will jump to help you by talking about the book, promoting it for you, and helping you find other opportunities.

Advertising

I used to think advertising was a sucker's bet. I ran a few ads on Goodreads and Facebook for one of my books, and they produced exactly nothing. After that, I concluded that the whole advertising scene was a waste of money.

It's true that there are a lot of ways to waste money on ads and have them not work. But, when done right, advertising is a power tool that can get you sales at a profit, with far less work and far more scalability than other options for spreading the word about your book.

Here's the experience that completely reversed my opinion on ads. One of my clients wanted to release a book to help him get clients for his business. The only problem is, he had no fans, no mailing list, and no relationships with influencers. He also didn't do any guest posting, interviews, or PR.

About the only option we had to sell his book was advertising, so we bought some ads. He spent only $137.84 on his launch ads:

- $29 for a BuckBooks non-fiction ad

- $40 for a BookSends ad for non-fiction at priced 99 cents

- $5 for a BKnights promotion

- $10.91 in Amazon Sponsored Product ads

- $52.93 in BookBub ads targeted to authors of related books

Those ads and a little word of mouth got him to #2 bestseller. He was in the top 10 for seven different categories. That's the power of ads.

Not only that, but as we kept running well-targeted Book-

Bub ads after his launch, he stayed on the bestseller charts day in and day out, week after week. Royalties from books sales were paying for the ads while his book kept bringing him new leads for his business.

For your launch, I recommend using the same services:

- BuckBooks

- BookSends

- BKnights

- BookBub Ads

- Amazon

Here's a little bit of information on each one.

Buck Books

This site is dedicated to promoting books priced at 99 cents, which is the price I recommend for your launch.

The requirements are:

- Priced at 99 cents, or free for non-fiction

- 60 pages or more

- professionally designed cover

- sales copy well written and proofread

- at least 10 reviews with an average of 3.8 stars or higher

The pricing for this service is $9 for fiction or $29 for non-fiction. When you're ready, you can apply here: http://buckbooks.net/promotions/

BookSends

This service also advertises discount books to their email subscribers, who have signed up to be notified about deals on books. The requirements are:

- At least 5 reviews with a high average rating

- Sale price less than $3 and at least 50% off of full price

- Lowest price the book has been in the past 90 days

They have targeted lists for different genres, with pricing at $40 for non-fiction, $20-60 for adult fiction, and $10 for children's books. When you're ready, you can apply here: https://booksends.com/advertise.php

BKnights

This is a Fiverr gig for promoting discounted books on BKnights's website (5,500 unique visitors per day) and email list (50,000+). When you're ready, you can apply here: https://www.fiverr.com/share/4KZbR

Amazon

Amazon offers an advertising service where you can promote your books, both fiction and non-fiction. You can sign up for an account from your KDP dashboard after you publish your book.

They offer sponsored product ads, which appear in search results and on the pages for other books. They also offer lockscreen ads, which appear on Kindle devices when they're inactive. I recommend choosing sponsored product ads.

When you set up Amazon ads, you can use automatic targeting, or you can use your own keywords. I recommend setting up at least one ad with each type of targeting.

With Amazon ads, the general strategy is to test as many keywords as you can think of. Most of the keywords won't do anything—your ad won't even run for them. A few may waste money, and a few may make sales. As you watch your ads over time, you'll want to eliminate the money-wasters and keep finding more keywords that make money.

For most people, the main difficulty is getting Amazon ads to run enough to make any difference, so the more keywords you can test, the better. I recommend using a tool like Publisher Rocket, but if you don't have that, you can try Google's Keyword Planner.

For these ads, you'll set a daily budget for the duration of your campaign. You can run these ads just during your launch, or you can start them before launch week and possibly get some early sales. Just be aware that most Amazon ads actually spend far less than their budget.

BookBub

BookBub serves both fiction and non-fiction, and their power lies in the ability to target specific authors. For example, if your book is very similar to the *Pretty Little Liars* franchise, you could target your ads to Sara Shepard's readers. If it's more like *7 Habits of Highly Effective People*, you can target Stephen Covey's fans.

The ability to target that closely means that very little of your ad budget is wasted on people who wouldn't be interested in your book. That's why BookBub ads are so effective, and they have a big enough audience that you can scale them up. If you want more sales, you can run more ads and have a good chance of achieving your goal. None of the other services offer that ability.

These ads run at the bottom of the emails of BookBub's

featured deals, so they reach the same audience as a BookBub Feature, just with less-desirable placement.

Another difference with BookBub is that you actually need to create a graphic to run your ad. BookBub's platform will generate one for you automatically from your book cover, but a graphic designed by a human is more likely to stand out and entice people to buy.

Whether you're writing fiction or non-fiction, at a minimum, your ad should include your cover, your special launch pricing, and a "Buy now" button. The button isn't actually real—no matter where readers click on your graphic, it will take them to your book's sales page—but having something that looks like a button helps guide people to click.

I recommend asking your cover designer to design your BookBub ad for you at the same time they do the cover, for a small additional fee. Another option is doing it yourself in PhotoShop or a free tool like Canva.

To sign up for BookBub ads, claim your author account here:
https://partners.bookbub.com/users/sign_up?form=partner_type
Then apply for an ad account once your author account is approved.

Building on the Book

One great thing about publishing a book is that it brings you many opportunities that can help feed book sales, which in turn bring you more opportunities. One obvious way for this to happen is through speaking. Many speakers publish books specifically so that they can get more speaking gigs and charge more when they speak. If you're interested in speaking, look for opportunities to speak on the topic of your book. Even giving a free talk may get you other speaking opportunities as well as back-of-the-room sales as people buy your book after your speech.

You can also use all of these opportunities to build your fan base. When you speak, invite people to sign up for your email list or Facebook page. You can offer them an incentive such as special content or exclusive discounts. Or, even if you don't want to offer anything, some people will still sign up. Give them that opportunity. The more fans you gather, the easier it will be when you need supporters for your next project.

Another way to build on your book is to offer offshoots in different forms. If you wrote a non-fiction book, can you offer a course or hands-on program to help your readers take the next step? Can you offer a service where your readers can hire you to complete the steps in your book for them? Can you host an intensive in-person experience where you take your readers through the process described in your book?

If your book is fiction, it may not make sense to offer a course or a program, but could you tell the story in a different form, such as a radio play, a comic book or a short movie? Think of all the ways companies have managed to create experiences based on extremely popular books like the *Harry Potter* series. How could you adapt similar ideas to your book to create an unforgettable experience for your fans?

As you're thinking of ways to build on your book, don't forget the most obvious: more books! After reading your first book, what will your readers want next? If you're not sure, ask them.

Now that you've written and published your first book, you

know what to do. You have knowledge and experience. You even have fans! It only gets easier from here. Whatever direction you take next, I wish you the best of success.

Action Steps

- Go back through your book description and make it as strong as possible.

- Approach fans, friends, family, bloggers, and Amazon reviewers to request honest reviews of your book.

- Revisit your ideal reader and make a list of blogs, podcasts, and other media you could use to reach him or her.

- For each possible venue, come up with three ideas that represent an overlap between the content of your book and the theme of that venue. Contact the editor or host and pitch your ideas.

- Keep your fans informed of these appearances so they can benefit from what you're sharing.

- Use press releases to promote your book to local media.

- Look for ways to build on the book. What do you want to offer next?

If you haven't already downloaded the workbook, don't forget to grab it. You can download all of these action steps and questions in one handy PDF at https://project-bestseller.com/resources.

Want More?

I hope this book has demystified the publishing process for you and given you the tools and direction you need to finish and publish your book. If you're a do-it-yourselfer, then I encourage you to go forth and conquer! I got into this business through trial and error on my own books. I did it, and you can, too.

On the other hand, if you'd like a little more support and guidance, you might want to check out the programs and e-courses I offer, including how to launch your book to bestseller and how to publish a book to bring in leads for your business. You can learn more about those in the Bestseller DIY School:

Project-Bestseller.com/school/

I also offer editing and design services to select customers. You can get more information on that at the Project Bestseller website (Project-Bestseller.com). I often have a waiting list for these services, but I'd love to work with you if it's a good fit.

Also, don't forget to check out the Resources section at the end of this book. There are a lot of details that I couldn't include here, and the Resources section will help you fill some of those in.

Good luck in your publishing endeavors. I wish you the best of success!

Acknowledgements

To my publishing clients, especially Gail Hand, Ann Ward, Leslie Stewart, Darius Willis, Leonard Zerman, Ari Meisel, S. Hopkins Adams, Murry J. Evans, Beth Niebuhr, Robert Hodam, Neil Grimmett, Glenn Gow, Jennifer Pinkley, Abraham Falls, Buddy Eades, and Rhonda Edwards: I've learned a lot from each of you. Thank you for everything you've shown me. I literally could not have written this book without you.

To my literary friends, especially Lynsey Bronaugh, Jeremy Bronaugh, Chuck Manley, Logan Wynn, Kimberly Casey, and Dave Trueb: thanks for all the inspiration and peer pressure! You guys are the ones who got me writing again. I can't thank you enough for that.

To the people who have mentored, guided, and inspired me, especially Jonathan Mead, Ash Ambirge, Lachlan Cotter, Tyler Tervooren, Mary Jaksch, Brené Brown, Marie Forleo, Felicia Spahr, Jonathan Fields, Leo Babauta, Tim Ferriss, Chris

Guillebeau, Adam Baker, Karol Gajda, Jenny Blake, Brian Tracy, Victoria Pennington, and many, many others. You opened up the world for me.

To everyone who gave me early feedback for this book, especially Emily Sprague Pardee, Greg Korbut, Logan Wynn, and Jessica Fiedorowicz. Your comments and suggestions have helped me immensely!

To Vanessa Hill, my editor and so much more. Thank you for your contributions to this book, and thank you for your work on all of these projects, past and future. Thank you for the countless mistakes you've caught and the infinite ways you've made our clients' books better. Most of all, thank you for supporting me through the dark times and keeping the business running when I couldn't.

To Elise, Jim Pierce, and Gaslight Anthem: you each helped me heal in your own way. I never could have made it through the past two years without you. Thank you.

To all of my friends and family, especially Al and Belinda Stein, Dani Stein, Jessica Fiedorowicz, Kathy Thomas, Sandy Ellis, Elizabeth Seifried, Jason Cookingham, Greg Korbut, Evans Criswell, Frances Akridge, Eric Jones, Doug Roth, Chandler Hall, and Geri Ewing: thanks for listening, supporting me, helping me through the bad times, and sharing the good. I love you all.

Finally, to Rick Martindale: you believed in me before I did. Not only that, you invested in my dreams and made my editing and design business possible. I can't thank you enough for that. Thank you for everything you taught me, through the good times and the bad. Thank you for loving me, sharing yourself with me, and showing me how utterly wonderful life can be. I'll never forget you.

Resources

Building Your Author Platform

Wordpress.com (one easy way to set up your website) https://wordpress.com

SiteGround (one of many inexpensive website hosting services, if you decide to host your own website instead of using Wordpress.com) https://www.siteground.com

Free Themes for WordPress https://wordpress.org/themes/

MailChimp (email list service, free for up to 2,000 subscribers) http://mailchimp.com

ConvertKit (a more robust email list service) https://convertkit.com

Writing and Finishing Your Book

Scrivener (writing software) http://www.literatureandlatte.com/scrivener.php

On Writing by Stephen King

Bird by Bird by Anne Lamott

Bestseller by Celia Brayfield

Fiction Unboxed by Sean Platt and Johnny B. Truant

Tactical Storytelling: One writer's guide to finishing the first draft by C. Steven Manley

Write. Publish. Repeat. by Sean Platt and Jonny B. Truant

No Plot? No Problem! by Chris Baty

The Dip: A Little Book that Teaches You When to Quit by Seth Godin

Do the Work by Steven Pressfield

The Mental Game

Uncertainty: Turning Fear and Doubt into Fuel for Brilliance by Jonathan Fields

The Big Leap: Conquer Your Hidden Fear and Take Life to the Next Level by Gay Hendricks

Maximum Achievement by Brian Tracy

The Power of Full Engagement: Managing Energy, Not Time, Is the Key to High Performance and Personal Renewal by Jim Loehr

Daring Greatly: How the Courage to Be Vulnerable Transforms the Way We Live, Love, Parent, and Lead by Brené Brown

Hiring an Editor

Editorial Freelance Association's list of editorial rates
https://www.the-efa.org/rates/

Venues and Tools for Publishing

For sales on your own website:

PayPal (transaction processing for sales from your website)
https://www.paypal.com/home

E-Junkie (basic shopping cart system for sales from your website) http://www.e-junkie.com/ej/pricing.htm

SamCart (full-featured shopping cart and sales page builder)
https://www.samcart.com

Fulfilled by Amazon (if you want to sell print books from
your website but not have to ship them)
http://services.amazon.com/content/fulfillment-by-amazon.htm

eBook, paperback, and audiobook distribution:

KDP (Kindle Direct Publishing for Kindle and print on demand) https://kdp.amazon.com

IngramSpark (print on demand)
https://www.ingramspark.com

Lulu (print on demand) https://www.lulu.com

Smashwords (eBook distribution)
https://www.smashwords.com

Draft2Digital (eBook distribution) https://draft2digital.com

ACX (Audiobook Creation Exchange) https://www.acx.com

ISBNs and barcodes:

Bowker ISBN service https://www.myidentifiers.com/Get-your-isbn-now

Free ISBN Barcode generators:

http://www.creativindiecovers.com/free-online-isbn-barcode-generator/

http://www.terryburton.co.uk/barcodewriter/generator/

Intellectual property protection:

U.S. Copyright Office http://copyright.gov

U.S. Patent and Trademark Office (for checking whether a trademark is already registered by someone else) http://www.uspto.gov/trademarks-application-process/search-trademark-database

Formatting Your Book

EPUB Straight to the Point: Creating eBooks for the Apple iPad and Other ereaders by Elizabeth Castro

Kindle Formatting: The Complete Guide To Formatting Books For The Amazon Kindle by Joshua Tallent (Some of the details in this are outdated, but the basics are the same)

Smashwords Style Guide - How to Format Your Ebook by Mark Coker

The Book Designer (offers tons of free information, as well as templates you can buy for your book interior) http://www.thebookdesigner.com

Marketing and Selling

Write to Sell by Andy Maslen

How to Write a Sizzling Synopsis: A Step-by-Step System for Enticing New Readers, Selling More Fiction, and Making Your Books

Sound Good by Bryan Cohen

Selling for Success: The Ultimate Guide to Developing a "Sales" Mindset, Selling in a Strategic Way, and Making The Impact You Want Your Life to Have by Felicia Spahr

Advertising for books:

Amazon Marketing Services (pay per click, delivered to shoppers on Amazon): sign up from your KDP dashboard once you've published your book

Free course on how to use Amazon ads effectively, presented by Dave Chesson of Kindlepreneur
http://17000-days.com/amz_ads

BookBub Ads (pay per click or pay per impression, delivered to email subscribers who have signed up to be notified about book deals) (not to be confused with BookBub features, which are highly competitive and require a significant up-front investment) Sign up at the address below to claim your author account, then apply for an advertising account.
https://partners.bookbub.com/users/sign_up?form=partner_type

BuckBooks (for new releases priced at 99 cents or free)
http://buckbooks.net/promotions/

BookSends (email promotion for discounted books)
https://booksends.com/advertise.php

BKnights (Fiverr gig for promoting discounted books on BKnights's website and email list)
https://www.fiverr.com/share/4KZbR

About the Author

I'm Cara Stein. I'm a book designer and editor. I'm also a writer.

In my publishing business, I help clients finish and publish their books, from writing and editing to formatting, typesetting, cover design, and marketing. (Learn more at Project-Bestseller.com.) I've taken over 200 books through publication.

I recently published my own coloring book for grownups called *Relax and Color*. I've also written and published three other books: *How to be Happy (No Fairy Dust or Moonbeams Required)*, *Getting Unstuck*, and *Reclaim Your Love*.

I've always wanted to be a writer, but I took a roundabout way of getting here. Among other relics of career change and self-reinvention, I have a PhD in computer science, assorted programming skills, several years' teaching experience, and advanced skills in wasting a whole afternoon surfing the internet.

I live in Huntsville, Alabama, with one stripy gray kitty cat.

Made in the USA
Monee, IL
01 September 2023

41963107R00063